*Bunratty: Rebirth of a Castle*

# BUNRATTY
## *Rebirth of a Castle*

BERNARD SHARE

First published in 1995 by
Brandon Book Publishers Ltd
Dingle, Co. Kerry, Ireland

© Bernard Share, 1995

British Library Cataloguing in Publication Data
is available for this book.
ISBN 0 86322 206 4

*Bunratty: Rebirth of a Castle* is published with the support of
Roadstone Provinces Ltd, a CRH Group company.

Photographs courtesy of Shannon Development (pp.25, 46, 50, 126,
146, 153, 158, 159, 173); the Office of Public Works (pp.109, 114, 115,
119, 120, 122, 131, 138, 139, 147, 182) and Seamus Kearns (p.69)

Front cover illustration: 'The Construction of Bunratty Castle'
by Dean van Jaeger. Back cover photograph The Slide File, Dublin.
Cover design: Peter Staunton, Tralee, Co. Kerry
Typeset by: Brandon
Printed by ColourBooks Ltd, Dublin

# Contents

# *Foreword*

IN NOVEMBER 1993 I was privileged to be present at the celebrations marking the thirtieth anniversary of the Mediaeval Banquets in Bunratty Castle. It was some time during the course of that excellent and extended entertainment that the idea for this account of the restoration of the castle was suggested to me by Cian O'Carroll, Chief Executive, Shannon Heritage & Banquets. He had, he told me, recorded on tape some years previously the recollections of many of those involved in the enterprise, and wondered whether there might be a book in it. The suggestion immediately appealed to me because I had been deeply impressed with what had been achieved at Bunratty ever since I had wandered into it, almost by accident, early in the 1960s when, on a quiet Sunday morning and with no other visible human presence, I experienced a profound sense of having missed the departure of the Great Earl of Thomond and his retinue by minutes. Thirty years later, when I again explored the castle at it lay apparently deserted on a rainy winter's morning, I was pleasantly surprised to discover that more than a hint of that distant and disconcerting awareness remained.

'So many build castles,' said Eochu in the 8th century *Voyage of Bran*, 'that they do not all find room in my memory.' That Bunratty is, in my view, well worthy of memorialising is due to the unique circumstances that led to its imaginative – and controversial – restoration and the involvement in that restoration of a group of individuals who, brought together by chance and circumstance, deployed their diverse tastes and talents to create, from the ruins of the past, something which has proved to possess enduring validity and meaning for the Ireland of today.

My deepest debt of gratitude, not only for the initial suggestion but for kindly and ready advice and assistance throughout the project, is to Cian O'Carroll. The narrative of the restoration owes much to the tapes he had the foresight to have made, and these I have supplemented with my own interviews. My thanks go to Jack Harrison and Barry O'Reilly, who planned and conducted the original interviews, and to all those who readily consented to affording me the benefit of their experience and recollections. I trust they will accept this as a grateful acknowledgment of their invaluable contribution.

My best thanks are also due to Paul MacMahon, Senior Architect at the Office of Public Works, Dublin, who allowed me access to the Board's files and to reproduce material therefrom. For assistance in the field of documentary research I am also indebted to the Director of the National Archives and Ms Rena Lohan; the staff of the National Library of Ireland and the Library and Manuscript Room of Trinity College, Dublin; Paddy Kilmartin and Padraig Gallagher of Shannon Development; Marcus Ó hEochaidh; Tom Sheedy of Bunratty Castle & Banquets. Leslie Matson assisted me with translations and Cian O'Carroll and Norman Mongan read and criticised the final draft. As always in these matters, however, the responsibility for any errors or omissions remains mine alone. Finally, this book would not have seen the light of day without the enthusiasm and encouragement of my agent, Jonathan Williams, and the work of Peter Malone at Brandon Book Publishers.

For the illustrations I am very largely indebted to Dermot Hurley of the Photographic Department of Shannon Development; to Marcus Ó hEochaidh; Cian O'Carroll; the Office of Public Works and Seamus Kearns.

*Bernard Share, Na Solláin, March 1995*

# A Cold Coming

IN VEVEY, ON the shores of Lake Geneva, the black marble slab on the wall of the church of St Martin memorialises Edmund Ludlow, in formal capitals, as HYBERNORUM DOMITOR. This conqueror of the Irish, who became the effective commander of the English army in Ireland following Henry Ireton's death in 1651, had subsequently refused to recognise the Protectorate and retired from public life in 1655. With the restoration to the throne of Charles II even such a withdrawn existence in his own country became untenable – he had been one of the signatories of Charles I's death warrant – and he fled into exile in Switzerland. There, in the hospitable Canton of Bern, in a house that was later to become the Hotel du Lac, he sat down, like many a rusticated military man before and after, to write a book.

As he wrote he was constantly on his guard against the precipitate appearance of enemies from Ireland or England bent on settling old scores. But Lieutenant-General Ludlow died peacably in 1692, and his *Memoirs*, 'printed at Vivay in the Canton of Bern, 1698', (though probably, in fact, produced in London), were dedicated 'To their excellencies The Lords of the Council for the Canton of Bern' for 'having been the Protectors of the Author of these Memoirs during the many years of his Exile'. Like many books of its kind, Ludlow's memoir is part political justification, part plain soldier's account: the record of a conscientious and competent soldier who through no real fault of his own ended up in the wrong country and on the wrong side.

Ludlow had taken part in the five-month siege which led to the fall of the city of Limerick to the English Parliamentary forces of Deputy Henry Ireton in October 1651. With the city and its starving, disease-ridden inhabitants secured, Ireton held a council of war to decide whether or not to march immediately on Galway, but winter was upon them and his officers complained that sickness and hard service had taken too great a toll of the men. Instead the Deputy ordered Edmund Ludlow across the Shannon into County Clare 'to reduce some places in those parts'. He set off at the head of about 2,000 foot soldiers and 1,500 cavalry for Clare Castle, but night overtook them. As they were crossing the bridge before the town the horse carrying Ludlow's medical supplies fell into the river, 'which proved a great loss to me, as things fell out afterwards'. The next day he negotiated the surrender of Clare Castle, but, forced to spend a miserable night in a tent on a hill, developed a bad chill, severe enough for his Adjutant-General to urge him to relinquish his command. Ludlow's response was to put a fur coat over his uniform, 'and an oiled one over that'. The next night, lying on his camp bed in an Irish cabin, he broke into a violent sweat which continued through the following bitter day, 'the wind and the hail beating so violently in our faces that the horses being not able to endure it, often turned about'.

Edmund Ludlow soldiered on, however, negotiating the surrender of Carrigaholt and placing a garrison there. He was making his way back towards Limerick when he met Ireton, who was coming to evaluate the situation for himself and 'to let us see that he would not command any service but such as he was willing to take a share of himself'. In unremitting hail and snow, the two set out to inspect possible winter quarters, entering the barony of the Burren, 'of which it is said that it is a country where there is not water enough to drown a man, wood enough to hang one, nor earth enough to bury him' – though Ludlow observed in passing that in spite of these conditions the cattle were very fat. They found Leamaneh, a castle of Conor O'Brien, 'whom we had killed near Inchecroghnan', well suited to their strategic purposes, put a garrison into it 'and furnished it with all things necessary'. By this time Henry Ireton had fallen seriously ill, and Ludlow, though still far from recovered himself, offered to accompany his commander back to Limerick. However, he wrote, 'so much more care did he take of me than of himself, that he would not suffer it; desiring me to go that day, being Saturday, and quarter at Bunratto, a house of the Earl of Thomond's, in order to recover my health, and to come to him on Monday morning at Limerick'. Ireton's illness – the plague, contracted from the stricken populace of Limerick – was to prove fatal; but the hospitality of Bunratty Castle proved the saving of Edmund Ludlow, who took over its command and who, two years later, was to experience a longer period under its substantial roof.

On 12 May 1277, some four hundred years before Ludlow was to spend his restorative weekend at the castle, an earlier Bunratty has gained a somewhat different reputation for hospitality. Brian Rua, Prince of Thomond, was the honoured guest of Thomas de Clare, the Anglo-Norman who had the previous year been granted the whole land of Thomond by England's King Edward I and who built at Bunratty 'a castle of dressed stone, girt with thick outer wall, containing a roofed impregnable donjon and having capacious white-lined appurtenances'. De Clare's writ, in fact, ran little further than the barony of Bunratty Lower, and he depended upon exploiting the rivalries of the various factions of the O'Briens to maintain his foothold. Hence the invitation to Brian Rua, and what followed.

Writing to Pope John XXII in the year 1317, a generation after the event, a number of Irish princes expatiated on 'the English inhabiting our land, who call themselves of the middle nation [but] are so different in character from the English of England and from other nations that with the greatest propriety they may be called a nation not of middle but of utmost perfidy. For, from of old they have had this wicked unnatural custom... when they invite noblemen of our nation to a banquet, during the very feast or in time of sleep they mercilessly shed the blood of their unsuspicious guests, and in this way bring their horrible banquet to an end.' It would appear that in Ireland the English did not have exclusive claim to this particular manifestation of hospitality, but the fate of Brian Rua was clearly considered a barbarism even by the rough standards of the day. De Clare, according to the princes' letter, 'suddenly tore him from the table and the feast, had him dragged at horses' tails, and having cut off his head had his headless corpse hung by the feet from a beam'.

The year following the dispatch of this letter of protest, Richard de Clare, son of Thomas, was involved in peace talks with King Murtagh O'Brien, son of Turlough and grand-nephew of the man his father had so summarily murdered. The meeting was held in the city of Limerick in May 1318, and from the start the new occupant of Bunratty showed himself in no mood to accommodate his enemies. Finally the Irish chiefs rode away across the Cratloe Hills to Tulla, murder in their hearts, whilst de Clare set off down river in the spring evening to return to his castle. A few months later he was dead, killed in bloody battle with the O'Briens, and Bunratty, in the words of the chronicler, lay 'deserted, empty, wrapped in fire'.

This series of swiftly receding images leads Bunratty's history back to its origins, in the Viking invasions of the 9th and 10th centuries. Looking at the beautifully shaped and proportioned hull of the Gokstad ship in the Oslo Viking museum, it is not difficult to envisage her at the head of the fleet battling its way up the Shannon estuary, fighting the villainous short seas produced by the confrontation of incoming tide and riverine outflow, the jaws of the menacing, blind-eyed animal headpost open as if baying for blood. The modest draught of these great vessels would have carried them – with the application of some not inconsiderable navigational skills – through the sandbanks and rocky hazards of that tortuous channel into the broad expanse above the future site of Limerick and onwards and upwards to Clonmacnoise and the rich booty of the Celtic monasteries.

What began as opportunistic raiding was consolidated into long-term settlement, and if the Vikings cannot be entirely transmogrified into an invasion force more devoted to rates and taxes than rape and pillage, as some revisionist historians have been moved to suggest, recent excavations in their 10th-century city of Limerick indicate a more stable and substantial civil community than had been conjectured heretofore. If they did nothing else, these entrepreneurial Norsemen confirmed the Shannon and its estuary as a vital communications link both for commerce and war. A thousand years on, the river with its estuary remains an important waterway, and one that still demands a degree of navigational skill and knowledge. 'Anchorage may be obtained off the entrance to Maigue river,' says the *Irish Coast Pilot*, 'in a depth of 3 fathoms, with Bunratty castle, situated about 7 cables northward of Quay island, in line with the eastern extremity of that island, bearing 354°.'

The view of the castle from the river makes it abundantly clear why possession of the site held the key to the military and strategic control of the hinterland and what was then Thomond and is now the county of Clare. Nothing could, or indeed can, move up and down river between Limerick and the sea without being observed from the high walls of Bunratty. The island, on which successive fortifications were raised, was virtually unassailable, accessible by land only by means of a track along the esker ridge from Sixmilebridge. All around it lay water and waterlogged marshland from which there emerged small and treacherous islets, appearing and disappearing with the tide. Richard de Clare, on that bitter voyage back from his Limerick encounter, would have needed a degree of skill in handling a boat and a sound knowledge of the tides to bring him to a safe mooring on the River Raite virtually under the castle walls.

Over three centuries later, Sir William Penn let go his anchor some distance offshore. In command of a substantial naval squadron, he had been sent by the English Parliamentarians to garrison Bunratty – then held by the fence-sitting Barnaby, Sixth Earl of Thomond – against the expected attack of the Irish Confederates. Barnaby acted in the tradition of equivocal Bunratty hospitality: 'His lordship,' an English settler, John Ward, complained, 'divers times entertained with meat, drink and lodging the most notorious rebels in all that country, and all that come are freely welcome.' A year before Penn's arrival on the 11 March 1646, Bunratty had been described as 'a port to master all ships'. He prudently came up river, however, in a small vessel, having left his command, the frigate *Peter*, moored off Glin, and was hospitably invited to dine with His Lordship of Thomond.

A few days later, on 20 March, Penn's journal records that 'Our pilot having informed my admiral that we might go up with our ship as high as Bonratty within two or three cables' lengths, at five fathom at low water... I caused our men to weigh about 5 in the morning... He, being as ignorant of the channel as impudent not to confess so much... laid our ship upon the top of a ledge of rocks six foot high. The tide being gone, we went round about her, with which lying she beat in a piece of plank in the bildge above 2 inches'. Eventually rescued by one of his captains, he got off again at six in the evening 'and came to anchor near Bunratty about 8'. William Penn was thereafter wary of the Shannon hazards and careful to avoid any further compromising of his seamanship.

Penn failed in his mission to hold Bunratty, and the siege and capture of the castle by the Irish in 1646 proved to be the last turbulent event in the long history of the fortification of the island of Tradraighe. And as the tide of battle ebbed through the succeeding centuries, so did the waters of the Shannon, retreating in the face of the land reclamation of the late 18th century until Bunratty Castle no longer looked out upon its impregnable island. In 1804 the Studderts, who has succeeded the O'Brien Earls of Thomond as owners and occupiers, built a bridge over the Owenogarney River, extinguishing the last element of its insularity. 'It is the widest one-arch stone bridge in Ireland,' claimed Pa Crowe, who worked on the 1950s restoration of the castle, 'and 'twas built by my great-grandfather. My forefathers came from Bunratty and they were supposed to be involved in the restoration in the castle in the 17th century.' The inscription on the masonry reads:

BUNRATTY BRIDGE
Built by
Thos. Studdert Esqr.,

At his own expense,
and finished A.D. 1804
John Smyth, Archt. John Crowe, Mason.

'The bridge will be the next thing to go,' predicted the writer
Frank O'Connor gloomily in 1947. 'It is obviously going to get in
the way of a grand new concrete road to Shannon airport.' His
fears proved ill-founded: the concrete road was built in 1964 but
it crossed a brand new bridge downstream from the old. Both
were in turn bypassed in 1992 by a major realignment of the
N18, so that Bunratty now lay behind a triple barrier denying
access to the waterway which had sustained it as outpost of the
English, bastion of the Irish, fortress and refuge, home and
haven through the building, sacking and rebuilding of four distinct yet intimately related edifices. Each rebuilding had offered
its own justification, but there was a special sense in which the
last reconstruction could claim to be – in the words of Erskine
Childers, then in 1960 the responsible government minister and

*'The widest one-arch stone bridge in Ireland':*
*built by Thomas Studdert in 1804*

subsequently President of Ireland – 'a defiance of history and a demonstration of national resurgence'.

With the building of the 1804 bridge, the Bianconi Mail Coach, which left Limerick at 9.45 a.m., after the arrival of the Dublin Mail, was able to take the direct route to Bunratty: it had until then travelled via Sixmilebridge. The Bianconi stables, where horses were changed, was located on the site of the modern winery which produces mead for the castle banquets. The mail left again for Ennis, which it reached at 12.15 p.m., en route for Galway. 'The mode of travelling is pleasant as well as safe,' wrote the compulsive English traveller Mrs C. S. Hall. 'Generally the cars proceed at a rate to the full as rapid as that of the stage-coaches, and persons of the highest respectability travel by them.' In 1843, however, William Makepeace Thackeray, the English novelist, decided to hire transport of his own.

Thackeray had been told on leaving Limerick to look out for woods and robbers, but was disappointed. 'But if woods and robbers did not come up to my romantic notions,' he wrote in *The Irish Sketch-Book*, 'the old castle of Bunratty fully answered them, and indeed should be made the scene of a romance, in three volumes at least'; and proceeded to offer a specimen chapter. 'The historical part of this romance has been extracted from the guide book,' he explained, 'the topographical and descriptive portion being studied on the spot.'

His history is bunk, but for that Thackeray himself can hardly be blamed. 'The huge and imposing mass of the castle, with its lofty and frowning southern arch,' wrote George Macnamara in *The North Munster Archaeological Journal* in 1915, 'must deeply impress the least emotional traveller who passes that way; but he will enquire in vain for any reliable history of the building.' Thackeray's 'descriptive portion', however, offers an insight into the state of a once mighty edifice in what appeared on all the evidence to be the autumn of its days: 'A policeman shows you over it, halls, chapels, galleries, gibbets and all. The huge old tower was, until late years, inhabited by the family of the proprietor, who built himself a house in the midst of it: but he has since built another in the park opposite, and half-a-dozen "peelers", with a commodity of wives and children, now inhabit Bunratty. On the gate where we entered were numerous placards, offering rewards for the apprehension of various country offenders; and a turnpike, a bridge, and a quay, have sprung up from the place which Red Redmond (or anyone else) burned.'

Sometime in the mid-1870s the owner of Bunratty, Captain Richard Studdert RN, removed a load of rubbish from the upper hall of the crumbling castle and put over it an arched timber roof covered with tarred felt. He concreted the floor, leaving a shallow open channel in the centre corresponding to the gutter of the preceding roof, rainwater now being disposed of through a hole in the wall under the south window. After his death his widow cleared away the remains of the roof over the apartment known as 'The Ladies' Drawingroom' and put in a concrete floor, together with one on the eastern terrace. She also made the top of one of the towers fit to walk upon. These interim measures, a feeble gesture in the face of time but no doubt as much as the family could encompass, did little to arrest the slow but steady decay of a once great bastion. The 1895 *Through Guide to Ireland* summarily dismissed Bunratty as 'erected at the end of the 13th cent. by Thomas de Clare, son of the Earl of Gloucester, but now a constabulary depot'. In 1914 Thomas Studdert, High Sheriff of Clare, offered to hand over its ownership and preservation to the Board of Works, but the times were again out of joint. Subsequently, the newly independent Ireland was to find itself with more pressing concerns. As civil war was succeeded by international conflict and the struggling new state was hedged with economic stringency, the decline and fall of what was, in the eyes of many, a symbol of the former occupying power, appeared irreversible, even acceptable: 'To clothe Bunratty after all its idle years,' wrote Stephen Rynne in *All Ireland* (1956), 'is too much like the American practice of beautifying corpses.'

There were others, happily, who were thinking very differently; and even as Rynne wrote, and in defiance of history and of the natural order of change and decay, the corpse was about to rise and give utterance.

# Swordland

'**P**ERCY WAS INTERESTED because it was the last mediaeval castle on the way to New York', said the archaeologist Marcus Ó hEochaidh of the involvement of his colleague, Percy Le Clerc, in the 1950s restoration of Bunratty. For Robert de Muscegros, however, in the 13th century 'the mouth of the River Raite', as the name Bun Ráite signified, was not so much a stepping stone as a point of no return.

It is possible that de Muscegros had heard, or even read, of the 5th-century voyage of St Brendan to the Promised Land: the *Navigatio*, the record of the saint's account of what was most probably the first European sighting of the American continent, had been something of a best seller since its first appearance *c.*800. But it is unlikely that de Muscegros would have learnt much of the local version from the Irish themselves. The Normans, in their experience, were hopeless linguists: *balbh gaill* – dumb or stammering foreigners – was the popular designation. If he was more adept than most, there is no evidence for it, for these early invaders left scant written records of their comings and goings, and even less personal information about themselves.

The first Anglo-Norman to receive from the English monarchy a grant of the cantred of Tradraighe – the name of the island on which four castles were to stand – was an even more shadowy figure than Robert de Muscegros. Arnold Keting is recorded as having been involved in 1199 in a land deal, exchanging Tradry, as he would have written it, for the middle cantred of Corcobaskin.

The arrangement was probably not to his advantage, since Tradraighe was considered the best land in Thomond. At this time the Norman presence on the north bank of the Shannon was only a couple of years old. Donogh Cairbech O'Brien had invited them to help dispose of his enemies – the Macnamaras, the O'Quins and a good many more – and it was probably in return for this logistical support that he relinquished to them the overlordship of Tradraighe, assuming, no doubt, that this would be a temporary tactical inconvenience. The Irish in general were slow in learning to take the Normans seriously.

According to the political practice of the day, O'Brien was confirmed by the government in London as a quasi-tenant-in-chief in part of his former territories, whilst another part – the best – was reserved to the crown for disposal as it thought fit. It was thus that the Anglo-Normans gained a foothold in the key location in Thomond. The foothold, as it happened, proved to be something less than secure; but the old Gaelic order was decisively subverted. The confiscated territories became 'swordland': a vast area where, in modern terms, a state of emergency was virtually continuous and the only right was might.

Arnold Keting, having made his pioneering appearance, vanished from the record. In 1246 Tradraighe was granted to Robert de Muscegros at an annual rent of £30, remitted for two years to enable him to build a castle. The fact that he also received 260 oaks from the king's forests suggests that this first Bunratty was a modest, even temporary construction, essentially a wooden palisaded tower surrounded by a deep ditch or fosse – deep because a substantial quantity of earth had to be excavated to form the mound on which the tower, or bretesch, was built. The purpose was almost exclusively military, and the tower itself may have been partially prefabricated, designed for ease and speed of erection and transportation, if necessary, to another location. It is not surprising, therefore, that the present castle site contains few echoes and no evidence of this first ephemeral structure.

The probable site of this first Bunratty became the location in 1959 of the Shannon Shamrock Hotel. The antiquarian T. J.

Westropp, writing in the *North Munster Archaeological Society Journal* in 1915, suggested that it could be identified with the large rectangular mound which is still visible, and this remained the received opinion until the antiquarian John Hunt undertook a hurried, four-day excavation just before construction of the hotel commenced. He dug a trench four feet wide on top of the 70 ft x 45 ft mound, which is ten to twelve feet high from the centre to the west along an east-west line. He discovered layers of humus and a quantity of burnt charcoal before reaching the local boulder clay. Further investigation was more rewarding: 'Running parallel with the line of the mound and close to its lower border was a foundation, 2ft high, of brickwork, built with 2" brick, 18" wide. This was followed into the bank at the sides, and was of uniform height throughout the length exposed ... it appeared to be complete in height as originally built. This wall was well mortared and sat upon a stone and mortar foundation layer on the clay subsoil. There was a clay floor just below the highest course of brick.' Outside the line of the wall he found a very dense layer of black material sloping up the side of the mound.

From this evidence Hunt reached the conclusion that 'the red brick foundation is that of a building of 16th century date. The dwarf wall foundation presumably supported a timber con-structed building, probably the late Gothic or Tudor domestic form of timber with lath and plaster filling... .' This building, he suggested, was destroyed by fire and the mound was built up by digging a broad trench and throwing the spoil on the debris. 'Upon the mound so formed, some sort of wooden structure was erected. The evidence for this is seen in the dense black layer seen in the fosse and sloping up the side of the mound... . It seems highly probable that this mound is the gun emplacement mentioned by [Sir William] Penn as erected to defend the broad, deep channel of water then separating the castle from the high ground to the north.' A relic of the 1646 seige rather than the castle of de Muscegros? Opinion remained divided and even Hunt, perhaps, was not entirely convinced. 'Hunt interpreted it when it suited him as a gun emplacement,' said Marcus Ó hEochaidh, who carried out a further excavation in the 1960s when an extension to the hotel was planned. 'We found part of the palisade of the bailey trench more or less on the boundary line between the property of the castle and the Shannon Shamrock.'

The few artefacts that Hunt unearthed – an iron knife, fragments of a cooking pot and a glass wine bottle (at least there was eating and drinking in it) he dated to the 17th century, with the exception of a fragment of glaze stoneware possibly a century older. Neither excavation revealed anything that could be dated to de Muscegros, but the first Bunratty's furnishings and equipment were in any case likely to have been minimal. Such structures were designed for small numbers of picked men operating in hostile territory, and their role, unlike that of the subsequent and more solid stone castles, was more offensive than defensive. Far from the main Norman centres of power, their function was to engage in fairly constant low-intensity warfare, a technique long established among the invaders' Irish enemies.

These enemies, amongst whom the O'Briens and the Macnamaras were the two most powerful Thomond families, had inherited a very different concept of war. The local king not only led his forces in battle; but also took upon himself the responsibility for the economic well-being of his people. As the state papers of England's Henry VIII recorded it: 'Every Iryshe captaine defendeyth all the subgetes [subjects] and the comyn folke, wythin his rome [realm] fro their eneymyes as much as in hym is [as much as lies in his power].' In a terrain where economic prosperity would have been closely linked to successful cattle raids, 'to rob and spoil their enemies they deem it none offence', as Richard Holinshed observed in the 16th century, 'nor seeke anie means to recover their losse but even to watch the like turne'. Not so much formal warfare, therefore, as sequential guerilla actions, with alliances forming and dissolving and the warring factions frequently changing sides.

The Normans were thus to discover that there was no single enemy whose defeat would result in the conquest of the territory as a whole. Though the city of Limerick, founded by the earlier wave of Norse invaders, had been garrisoned by the Normans as early as the 1170s, their comprehensive conquest was to falter here across the river in the stark landscape of Thomond. They were reduced to adopting the native mode, setting one enemy against the other, playing both ends against the middle, forging temporary and advantageous alliances, fortifying and holding as the opportunity provided.

For this form of tactical engagement Bunratty proved an excellent base, and the functional military outpost grew in time into a substantial settlement. In 1253 de Muscegros was granted a licence for Bunratty fair, an annual event which began the day before the feast of St Bartholomew (24 August) and ran for five days, arguing a sizeable population which was also catered for by a weekly Thursday market. By 1287 the town numbered a population of 226 burgages – or tenures held of the lord of the manor. These first citizens of Bunratty were, or course, immigrants, like those of the new town of Shannon, to be similarly purpose-built seven centuries later. Some of the names, if not the provenance, of these early 'blow-ins' are recorded: Richard de Altoun, William Odusthyr, Walter Russell, Walter Flemying, Patrick de Layunperun, Nicholas de Inteberg, Maurice de Rochford, Henry Fuke. There are still Rochfords in Ireland and the Russells were to play a recurrent role in the later history of Bunratty; but what became of the Fukes and the de Layunperuns? Did they return, disillusioned immigrants, to wherever they had come from, or were they cut down in the wars, sieges and epidemics that ravaged their settlement?

The town itself, according to Marcus Ó hEochaidh, who excavated the site of the Rinuccini gardens at Bunratty for the Office of Public Works in 1964-67, would have been located on the hill on which the mediaeval church now stands, an area which has been much disturbed, from an archaeological point of view, by later building and gravel digging. An outpost of Anglo-Norman manorial administrative rectitude in an alien environment, with the journey to the urban attractions of Limerick safely to be made only by water, it nevertheless marked the establishment of Bunratty as a place to live, as distinct from a place from which to sally forth to battle: a place, as it was to remain, which a wide diversity of people were to call home.

Robert de Muscegros died some time in the mid-1250s and was succeeded by his son John, who served as Sheriff of Limerick from 1261-75. Following a brief period when it reverted to the English king, Bunratty was delivered to Thomas de Clare. This younger brother of the Duke of Gloucester and Lord of Kilkenny, who though well-connected was lacking a substantial patrimony, has been the source of some historical confusion. In spite of his name he had no association with the future county, which is generally considered to derive its name from the epony-mous village where a board, or *clár*, placed across the river Fergus, served as a bridge. In the 19th century one of the Studdert family was named Thomas de Clare because he was born in the castle – a *jeu d'esprit* which probably served to add a moiety to the confusion; the original de Clares, however, came quickly to be closely identified with the territories which had fallen to their lot.

On 26 January 1276 Thomas de Clare was granted the whole land of Thomond, including most importantly Bunratty, which the king had repossessed from the grandson of the first de Muscegros. When he had built this first 'castle of dressed stone', de Clare 'strengthened it and the precincts with a broad-based, high-crested rampart, with ditch running from the stream [the Raite River, now the O'Garney or Owenogarney] to the sea'. He instituted an early manifestation of ethnic cleansing: having expelled the existing inhabitants, he 'assigned that region to plebian English and the kerne of the Gael his allies, to squat there'. He then set about consolidating his position by exploiting Irish rivalries.

In spite of the five-day fair, life for the newly installed inhabi-tants of Bunratty town must have been a stressful experience. Attacks on the castle were frequent; an epidemic resulting from a seige in 1280 carried off many of the townspeople. Thomas de Clare, however, died, if not in his bed, then in similarly peaceful circumstances, in 1287. His son Gilbert was a minor, so the castle again reverted to the king's hand. In 1289 the Royal Escheator

was paid £11 10s. 8d. [£11.54 approx.] for repair and construction work which included a fosse and palisade round the castle
and a fosse and enlarged pool for the mill. Covering the large
tower and chamber near the river, raising a wooden tower
beyond the gate – which was also supplied with new locks – and
repairs to dwellings within the castle itself absorbed a further £5
3s. 9d. [£5.20 approx]. Whatever about the town, Bunratty Castle
had clearly assumed an importance which justified substantial
expediture: some £230 on maintenance, repairs and supplies
during the ten years from 1289 that it remained in the king's
hand.

The portraits of the Earls of Thomond which hang in the
restored castle seem at first glance to inhabit another world from
that of Richard de Clare and Brian Rua. The fourth or 'Great'
earl, Donough O'Brien, wears the Elizabethan ruff (he died in
1624) and above it the enigmatic smile of a man for all seasons.
Governor of Clare, Lord President of Munster, he had succeeded his father, Conor, the third earl, in 1580: four years later
the number of County Clare castles in the possession of the
O'Briens was estimated at forty-seven. The third earl's seat had
been at Clonroad Mor, Ennis; his successor chose, however, to
move to Bunratty and to improve and furnish it in a manner
befitting his rank and station.
   Donough's son and heir, Henry – from his portrait perhaps
both shrewd and humorous – was, as it transpired, overreached
in historical resonance both by his father and his younger
brother Barnaby, the sixth earl and the last to live in Bunratty. In
Barnaby's portrait, in which he seems constrained rather than
accommodated within a square frame marking the extremities of
a formal oval, his military armour forms an apposite contrast to
the scarf tied somewhat flamboyantly round his neck: his martial
qualities, as his contemporaries recorded, being tempered by an
abiding concern for his own person. His eyes are those of a man
alive to the main chance, but though in the verdict of history
both calculating and cowardly, Barnaby was nevertheless: 'A man
most potent and popular here,' Admiral Sir William Penn con-

*Donough, fourth or Great Earl of Thomond*

cluded in 1646, 'and so able to draw in, or keep back others, and they no mean ones, according to his own dispose and temper.' Barnaby's 'dispose and temper' were, to say the least, unpredictable; and perhaps in this characteristic if in no other he embodies those of his ancestors who, three hundred years before him, had enmeshed the calculating de Clares.

The portraits of the Earls of Thomond were offered on loan to the castle's trustees on its restoration by Sir Donough Edward Foster O'Brien, sixteenth Baron Inchiquin and head of a family which traces its origins to Brian Boroimhe, High King of Ireland in the 10th century, and which can boast a pedigree amongst the oldest in Europe. They owed their extensive hegemony to a somewhat insignificant tribe known as the Dál gCais, or Dalcassians, which appeared in the historical record in the early 10th century. It had invented for itself a pedigree according it a collateral line of descent from one of the semi-mythical invaders of Ireland, Mil, and through him to the dominant Eoghanacht dynasty. The rise of the Dál gCais and their descendants, the Ua

...ns, is one of the most remarkable events in Irish ... early example of a highly successful public rela-
...n.

...occupying an area east of the Shannon in what is now ... Limerick and north Tipperary, the Dál gCais had crossed the river some time in the 5th century and succeeded in detaching east Clare from Connacht, creating a new territory to become known as Tuadhmumu, ('north Munster') or Thomond. Through their spurious ancestry the tribe laid claim both to the kingship of Munster and the dominant kingship of Cashel, claims which they successfully reinforced in arms. The rise of one of their number, Brian Boroimhe, to the high-kingship of Ireland, and his adoption of the O'Brien name (literally 'son of Brian') for his many descendants saw the consolidation of their dominant role. The Macnamaras, or Mac Con Maras, who were both to share and dispute the territories of Thomond with the O'Briens, were after them the most important sept of the Dál gCais and served them as marshals.

Brian Boroimhe married at least four wives, with the result that from the earliest times the O'Brien family branches were both numerous and widely distributed. Their titles of nobility or election have included High King of Ireland; kings of Munster and Thomond; princes of Cashel and Thomond; The O'Brien; Governor of l'Ile de France; Comte de Thomond; Conde de O'Brien; Earls of Thomond, Clare, Inchiquin, Orkney; Marquess of Thomond; Marquis de Casteltomond; Baron Inchiquin, Baron of Castle Lyons, Baron Shannon of Cork, Baron de Castletomond; Knight of Calatrava; Knight of Santiago; Marshall Thomond, Marshall de France...

Several of the senior O'Brien titles, including the viscountcy of Clare, the earldom of Inchiquin and the earldom of Thomond, are now extinct. When the mediaeval banquets were established in the castle in 1963 invitations were issued in the name of 'the Earl of Thomond', a practice which quickly drew a protest from the then Lord Inchiquin. He wrote to the *Limerick Leader* pointing out that though the earldom was then extinct his family continued to hold title to it. Its use for promotional purposes, he complained, could lead to misunderstanding. On at least one occasion such proved to be the case. On attending a banquet while on an official visit to Ireland, Kenneth Kaunda, president of Zambia, was invited to occupy the earl's seat at the high table and preside over the festivities – an offer that was customary in respect of a distinguished guest. ('He played the guitar,' recalled Joe McElgunn of Shannon Sales and Catering, the organisation responsible for the castle management.)

Unfortunately, said McElgunn, Dr Kaunda was left with the impression that the rank and style of Earl of Thomond had been formally and irrevocably conferred upon him, and was with difficulty dissuaded from assuming it in perpetuity upon his return to Lusaka. Under the 1937 Constitution of Ireland, Article 40.2, 'No title or nobility of honour may be accepted by any citizen except with the prior approval of the Government.' It would have been ironic, to say the least, if the earldom of Thomond had been fortuitously reinstated in the heart of Africa.

In 1994 Conor O'Brien, eighteenth Baron Inchiquin of the Leamaneh or Dromoland branch, recognised as the main line of descent, was living in the territory, now County Clare, inhabited by his forebears for over a millenium. It was the younger son of an earlier Conor O'Brien, King of Thomond, that Thomas de Clare so treacherously and brutally disposed of at the banquet in Bunratty in 1277. There were several versions of what occurred, some no doubt drawing upon the imagination of whoever was telling the tale, but the central horror remains. According to one of the most graphic accounts, 'After they had exchanged mutual vows by the relics, bells and croziers of Munster, Thomas de Clare caused Brian to be drawn asunder between strong steeds until death released him.' Brian Rua's crime was not to have taken a firm enough line – in de Clare's view – with his nephew Turlough who was challenging him for the kingship. The Irish law of dynastic succession did not add to the security of the king's position, since every man whose father, grandfather or great-grandfather had held royal authority was considered, both by himself and others, to be 'material for a king'. It was a far cry from the rigorous Anglo-Norman legal system or '*Termes de la Ley*'.

Thomas de Clare found himself no more successful with Turlough than he had been with Brian Rua, and he quickly – and perhaps as an act of remorse – transferred his support back to the murdered Brian's son, Donough. In 1293 he held another Donough, Turlough's son, in Bunratty as a hostage; but in the spring of 1298 Turlough beseiged the castle. John le Marshall, clerk of the exchequer in Dublin, was obliged to allocate over a hundred pounds to pay armed foot and horse to accompany the Justiciar to raise the siege. It proved to be no more than a temporary relief.

The Macnamaras, chiefs of Uí gCaisin (approximately the present barony of Bunratty Upper) had held since 1099 the ancient privilege of naming the O'Brien kings at the ceremonial site of Magh Adhair, some three kilometres north-east of Quin. 'On the day of the inauguration,' wrote Fr Martin Ryan in The Other Clare (1977), 'the sub chiefs of the territory, and all the great officers of the State with the brehons, poets and historians, were present, as also the bishops, abbots and other leading ecclesiastics. The hereditary historian of the tribe read for the elected chief the laws which were to regulate his conduct, after which the chief swore to observe them, to maintain the ancient customs of the tribe and to rule his people with justice.' It was the Macnamaras who, in the closing years of the 14th century, at least twice burned Bunratty in an attempt to recover their forfeited lands.

Thomas de Clare's elder son Gilbert was recognised as having reached his majority in 1302 but died shortly thereafter and was succeeded in 1307 by his brother Richard. Richard was very much his father's son: the descendants of Teig and Brian O'Brien were again in hot dispute, and, assessing their relative strengths, he shrewdly decided to support the latter. However, another great Norman family, de Burgh or de Burgo, had formed an alliance with the opposing faction. On 20 May 1311 the forces of William de Burgo fought those of Richard de Clare on Bunratty Hill. De Burgo himself and some of his nobles and men were captured and held prisoner in the castle while Dermod O'Brien, Brian Rua's grandson, pursued the remnant back into Connacht from whence they had come.

De Clare, for the moment, had backed the winning side, but he was rapidly becoming the focus of a growing hatred on the part of all the Irish of Thomond. Among the ghosts which surely continue to haunt Bunratty are those of three Macnamara hostages, the eldest son of Mac Con and the two sons of Lochlainn, who were hanged in the castle in 1313. A fourth, Mahone, son of Cumedha Mór, was spared on the intervention of the clergy and after the payment of 90 marks (about £120). It is perhaps this last sordid financial transaction that most aptly epitomises Richard de Clare. The following year, during his absence in England, Bunratty was again burnt. In 1315, a year in which famine ravaged Ireland, he was awarded a hundred marks for his services against the Irish of Leinster, but it was from the enemies nearer home that he was to receive his quietus.

In 1318, after the unsuccessful peace process in Limerick, he with his allies decided to move against Murtagh O'Brien. First, however, they had to pass through the territory of the O'Deas of Dysert. As they were crossing the river Fergus, legend has it, de Clare and his army came upon an old hag washing armour and rich robes, blood from which was staining the water. On his enquiring of an Irish ally what this signified, he was told that it was the armour and clothing of de Clare himself and his entourage, and that they would not survive the battle. The interpretation proved true. The pitched battle took place, again according to tradition, near Corofin, Conor O'Dea being joined by Murtagh O'Brien and Maconmara; de Clare, with a small advance guard, was cut off and killed. His now leaderless and demoralised forces fled back to Bunratty, where on learning of her husband's death de Clare's wife Johanna set the castle and its towers ablaze and sailed off up river to the safety of Limerick, never to return. The remains of de Clare and his knights were given burial in St Francis' Friary in Limerick.

Deserted, empty, wrapped in fire... the Irish victory, for the moment, would seem to have been total. In 1321 it was recorded that 'The lands of the Lordship are waste and out of cultivation for the past three years; neither are there any free tenants or others dwelling in Thomond save only the Irishmen who dominate therein, with the exception of a few dwellers in the town, who are beginning to rebuild in the same town which was burned and destroyed on the day when the Lord Richard de Clare was slain, after whose death neither Englishman nor Irishman paid any rent or did any service.'

Surprisingly, Bunratty Castle itself would seem to have survived the holocaust better than might have been inferred from the foregoing account. In 1319 Edmund Hakelut, Escheator of Ireland, paid out £35 12s. 6d. (about £35.75) to five men at arms with five caparisoned horses, twelve hobelars (light horsemen) and seventy-eight foot soldiers as wages for thirty-eight days' duty, from 11 May, 'in garrison of Bonrat Castle, to protect it and the parts adjacent after the death of Richard de Clare.'

Two years later, on 26 May 1321, a survey found that 'the tower in the Castle has good walls but is unroofed and slighted [levelled – though this calls in question the state of the walls]. Beside it is a stone chamber with a stone filled cellar. Another chamber roofed with planks. A stone kitchen joined to the tower and chamber, with a cistern and an oven. The surrounding houses were ruined and of no value. The castle mill is of use only to the inhabitants squatting in the ruins. The whole of Thomond is worth nothing, being in the hands of the Irish.' It was to remain so for almost three centuries.

On 23 October 1915 *The Irish Builder* published an illustrated article on Bunratty. Though largely a reproduction of the contributions of George Macnamara and T. J. Westropp to the *North Munster Archaeological Journal* of the same year, it nevertheless took issue with those authorities on the matter of what might be termed the impacted essence of the successive buildings on the site. Of de Clare's castle it asserted that 'it must be observed that there has been no real discovery of its remains and foundations, such as we might reasonably expect in the case of so strong and famous a fortress, particularly, situated as the Castle is, in a rural district. It must have been not inferior in construction to Quin Castle, which he [de Clare] also built, and the towers of which still remain. Must it not have been on the site of the present castle?' Whilst this sense of physical continuity has a powerful emotive dimension, it remains at best unproven.

Thomas de Clare, Richard's son and the last male representative of the family, died in 1321. On 20 April of the following year, all their lands and castles were assigned to Robert de Welle. Some rebuilding must have taken place under this new assignee, for the castle was sufficiently habitable to house a constable who acted as the king's representative, de Clare's interest having reverted to the crown for want of a male heir. On 7 November 1325 the king's authority was flagrantly flouted by Maurice Fitz Thomas, subsequently the first Earl of Desmond, who urged four of his men to lay hold of Richard of Harmston, the constable of Bunratty, when he unsuspectedly left his charge to go into the village, and 'to cut out his tongue, gouge out his eyes and take over command of the castle'.

Whether in fact Harmston suffered this outrage is not clear, but any occupation must have proved temporary. Six years later, on 18 February 1331, Fitz Thomas (or Desmond, as he had now become) was inciting Sir John Fitzmaurice and others – amongst whom the Russells once more appeared in association with the fortunes of Bunratty – to capture the castle. They were still in possession on 20 August, when they commandeered a cask of wine from one Simon Duff 'and, when the earl came to the castle, he joined them in drinking it amid great jubilation'. The hospitable ambience of the castle was again reasserting itself. Desmond appointed John Fitzmaurice as constable, instructing him to withold obedience from the justiciar, or chief political officer under the Norman kingship, or from anyone else who remained loyal to King Edward III. Fitzmaurice had not long to profit from the new dispensation, however: the following year, 1332, in the month of July, Bunratty was attacked by the combined forces of the O'Briens and the Macnamaras and razed to the ground. As the Latin annals sombrely put it: '*Castrum de Bunrat capitur et ad terram prosternitur per Hibernicos...*'

To focus thus on the fortunes of one relatively minor Norman stronghold is, of course, to view Irish history through the wrong end of a telescope. This first Earl of Desmond, for example, who makes but a brief appearance in the Bunratty record, was to come close to destabilising Anglo-Norman rule throughout Ireland. The FitzGeralds, of whom he was one, traced their ancestry to the Gherardinis of Florence, and the earl was in a direct line from the Maurice FitzGerald who had been one of the key members of the first Norman invasion force in 1169. More Cambro- than Anglo-Norman, the Geraldines saw themselves as possessing an affinity with the Celtic Irish and thus as their logical rulers; and by the time of the first Earl of Desmond, they had more than once manifested their opposition to the English king.

The relative simplicities of late 20th century Irish politics, with their fixation on no more than two traditions, would have meant little to the Normans. Richard II assessed the situation in terms of 'the Irish rebels, the wild Irish, our enemies and the obedient English' – the Geraldines being numbered among the first category. Though some of them also gave the monarchy cause for concern on account of a tendency to become, in the well-worn phrase, *Hiberniores ipsis Hiberniis*, any tendency to embrace Irish ways was attributable not to any love of the 'wild Irish', who had for them no meaningful political existence, but to a perceived need to assert a distinctive identity. As with the Anglo-Irish of a later century, their fundamental concern was the maintenance of their personal power and property within the framework of loyalty to the monarchy, if not necessarily to its current representative or his servants in Ireland. Hence Desmond's instructions to John FitzMaurice to withhold obedience from the king's representative.

Edward III had sent over the new justiciar, Anthony Lucy, specifically to curb the 'home-rule' inclinations of the Geraldines and the other powerful families of Anglo-Ireland. He was only partially successful. When in 1341 Desmond, having served a period of imprisonment, resumed command of the Patriots, as they thought of themselves, and summoned his own parliament in Kilkenny, 'Never,' the annals recorded, 'was there so notable a division between the English by birth and the English by blood.' John FitzMaurice, Desmond's appointee, was also jailed – in his case for his part in the loss of Bunratty to the Irish. He was released on the orders of the king in September 1357 from Limerick Castle 'since there is insufficient evidence against him'. By this time in Tradraighe, another new castle had risen from the ashes of the old.

'It is improbable that there was much moulding or ornamental detail in a castle built by either Thomas or Richard de Clare,' suggested T. J. Westropp; 'however, no fragment of any earlier building is recognisable in the walls of Bunratty, nor do any foundations of towers appear in fields near it.' But, echoing the doubts expressed in *The Irish Builder*, those who were involved in the 1950s reconstruction were not so sure.

'Don't you think the lower part of the Castle at least must be 14th century?' its new owner, Lord Gort, wrote to Percy Le Clerc on 19 October 1957 as the work was well advanced. On 1 November Le Clerc replied, informing him that 'in the tunnel through the west wall we have found that the present enormous wall thickness is due, as I had suspected, to a second thickness of wall having been applied to the outside of an earlier wall. The earlier wall has a base batter and was therefore the external wall of something – probably a tower house'. Pa Crowe recalled digging down eight feet in the basement and coming upon what he took to be 'the ruins of the older castle'.

If these putative remnants hold any echo from the past it is likely to be that of a new justiciar, Sir Thomas de Rokeby, appointed in the summer of 1349, who undertook a campaign in the south-west in 1350-51. Bunratty, in the official view, was far too important strategically to be left in the hands of the Irish enemies; but before de Rokeby, who successfully occupied Munster and Thomond, could turn his attention to rebuilding it (or perhaps as the work was proceeding, as there is some uncertainty as to dates), another act of insensate violence took place, apparently within the precincts. In 1353 Roger Craddock, Bishop of Waterford, tried two Macnamaras of Clann Cuiléin for what was reported as 'an offence against Our Lady' – though it is possible that this was a trumped-up charge concealing some other motive. Since Bunratty lay within the diocese of Killaloe, Craddock was acting outside his jurisdiction and entirely without authority, but the two men were found guilty and burnt at the stake. Whatever the reason, the act was deeply resented: in consequence Roger Craddock's superior, the Archbishop of Cashel, attacked and despoiled the city of Waterford.

Whether this grisly event took place in de Rokeby's castle is not clear, but that structure, which was probably at best a hasty rehabilitation of what had stood before, was itself to meet a violent end, probably before it was even completed. On this occasion the destruction by the Irish was politically definitive: the English presence in Thomond was effectively extinguished and for the next 215 years the O'Briens and the Macnamaras were to hold the territory under native rule. Towards the middle of the 15th century Maccon Mac Síoda Mac Conmara (or Macnamara), chief of Clann Cuiléin, began to build at Tradraighe the fourth and final castle of Bunratty. 'It seems true, judging from the plans,' claimed *The Irish Builder*, 'that whatever happened earlier, the Irish who took de Rokeby's castle certainly either merely repaired it, or else rebuilt it on pretty much the same lines.' The evidence, if any, lies within and beneath the massive walls of what H. G. Leask, Inspector of National Monuments for the Office of Public Works, was to describe in his report in 1935 as 'quite the finest structure of its kind in Clare'.

# Lámh Láidir in Uachtar

In January 1581 Conor, third Earl of Thomond, died and was succeeded by his son Donough. For the inauguration of the new chief of the O'Briens the poet Maolin Óg Mac Bruaideadha composed an ode offering the traditional advice to a prince assuming his new responsibilities. The practice of the authorised laureate's pronouncing an hortatory ode before the elected king, prince or chieftain on his being enthroned was as old as Gaelic civilisation, and had survived the succession of the last King of Thomond by the alien earldom.

The bardic profession had risen from the ashes of the druidic order and its final manifestation – that of the court poet – was, as the scholar Osborn Bergin described it, 'a professor of literature and a man of letters, highly trained in the use of a polished literary medium, belonging to a hereditary caste in an aristocratic society, holding an official position by virtue of his training and learning, his knowledge of the history and traditions of his country and his clan'. But even as the 16th century bards (and their numbers were by no means negligible) devoted themselves to sustaining the fabric of the old Gaelic order, the foundations were being swept away from under their feet. Donough O'Brien was king only by courtesy. Conor, last King of Thomond under the old dispensation, had died in 1539, and on 1 July 1543 Henry VIII had created Murrough O'Brien first Earl of Thomond in return for his submission to the English crown.

*Lámh Láidir in Uachtar* – the strong hand uppermost: the traditional motto appeared on the O'Brien arms when they adopted the European heraldic conventions of the Norman invaders. Subsequently it was also rendered in Norman French: *Vigeur de Dessus*. The coat of arms was 'gules three lions passant guardant in pale or' and the crest 'a dexter arm embowed issuing out of a cloud and brandishing a sword all proper'. But the three gold lions on a red background also figured in the arms of the English monarchs, so the O'Brien felines, though permitted to retain their red ground, acquired hindquarters of silver and the new emblazon was now described as 'gules three lions passant guardant in pale per pale or and argent'. The new Earl of Thomond and his successors were, however, accorded the right of wearing the royal crimson liveries on (English) state occasions.

On 10 March 1520 Henry VIII had appointed Thomas Howard, Earl of Surrey, Lord Lieutenant of Ireland and two months later dispatched him with a thousand men and instructions to win the country over by 'sober waies, politique drifts and amiable persuasions'. That the conduct of this and subsequent military missions was to prove neither politic nor amiable was not entirely the king's fault, the Irish proving markedly reluctant to co-operate in this new expansion of power and the 'Old English' – the great and established families from an earlier era of colonisation – equally so. They had some reason, for, as the English historian Fynes Moryson was to complain, 'All the English in generall that voluntarily left England to plant themselves in Ireland, either under the sayd undertakers of Mounster, or upon the landes of any other English-Irish throughout Ireland, or to live in cittyes and townes, were generally observed to have been eyther papists, men of disordered life, bankrots, or very poore... by which of course Ireland... was made the sincke of England... .'

From 1534 England maintained a standing army in Ireland, but many of their number, who brought little political conviction to their designated role, deserted to the Irish camp, where their familiarity with modern military methods proved invaluable to their new employers. Others simply formed local liaisons and melted into the landscape. The Normans, three centuries earlier, had depended on Irish troops not only for intelligence but for manpower in battle. Now, as England's new westward expansion, which was to extend beyond Ireland to North America, gathered momentum, the battle-lines became once more racially blurred. Not only did the Irish fight as advantage offered for the New English, the Old English or themselves: they continued to fight each other. This often chaotic entanglement of allegiances led to representatives of the one family finding themselves in deadly opposition, not only espousing opposing causes but embracing conflicting religions. Notable amongst the divided septs were the Thomond O'Briens, who were to prove themselves particularly skilful at changing political and religious sides at the crucial moment. 'The brain reels,' as one historian put it 'in any attempt to define who were rebels and who were not at this particular time in Clare.'

For two centuries after the Norman invasion, architecture in Ireland had differed little in its broad essentials from that of the French and English. The Normans, according to Percy Le Clerc, had imported their own style and their own building organisation and even materials, including ready-carved and moulded stone. In the 15th century, with the Norman presence in Thomond marginalised, powerful families such as the Macnamaras and the O'Briens built themselves, in Le Clerc's words, 'a whole system of castles, big and small, in their territories; they were rich enough, moreover, to endow abbeys, to found friaries and to build numerous churches. Their building activity reached its peak during the third quarter of the fifteenth century and it is estimated that over two thousand castles were built... the period is remarkable for the very high quality of workmanship, for the originality of the architectural planning and for the elegance of design; we have, for the first time in Ireland, a systematic architecture... that is quite distinct from contemporary work in neighbouring countries.'

The fourth Bunratty Castle, begun by Mac Síoda Mac Conmara and completed by his son Seán Fionn, who died in 1467, passed into the hands of the O'Briens some time about 1500, though very little evidence of the transaction has survived. The less than explicit account of 'the Chevalier' O'Gorman[1], who wrote at the close of the 18th century, speaks of one 'John Finn Macnamara being obstructed by Donat Earl of Thomond, whose ancestors, no later than his father or grandfather, acquired the castle and lands of Bunratty some way or other by purchase from one Macnamara [Mac Conmara] that was inheritor thereof.'

This new Bunratty, however, was built to last. Harold Leask, sometime Inspector of National Monuments for the Office of Public Works, described it in his authoritative book *Irish Castles* (1941) as the finest of the great towers of Ireland: 'It is an oblong building, lofty, and furnished at each corner with a square tower or turret. A picturesque feature is the broad arch which unites the southern turrets just below the topmost storey and casts a bold shadow on the walls below... it is clearly a structure of the prolific later part of the XVth century... .'

'The structure of the castle is a logical architectural solution of defence problems,' the art critic of *The Irish Times* suggested on the occasion of its reopening in May 1960. 'The drawbridge entrance faces north to the homeground. Above this the single spiral staircase leads to the Great Hall of the Earl, easy for defence and scrutiny of entrants.' (The stair had a most unusual left-hand twist, thus impeding the thrust of a right-handed attacker from below while leaving the defender above a free sweep of his sword arm.) 'At the four corners of the Great Hall are placed the kitchen, the buttery hatch, the chapel and a robing room, and behind each of these, staircases leading to the upper floors. In fact, the four bays which flank the principle central section contain all the offices and services and defence points, while the basement store, the guardroom and the Great Hall, one above the other form the core of the castle.'

'The solidity of the masonry is quite incredible,' said Percy Le Clerc, who succeeded Leask in the office of inspector. 'In the fourteenth century the masonry is attractively designed but it isn't very solid; but in the fifteenth it is like best quality concrete.' And it was a truly lordly establishment, he added: 'How many houses of that size in the nineteenth century would have had sixteen WCs?'

Before Murrough's submission the English had regarded the possession of Bunratty as essential to their plans to secure their power base in Ireland. In 1536 one Robert Cowley wrote to Secretary of State Thomas Cromwell that he intended to produce 'a little treatise concerning the re-adoption of the King's dominion in Ireland and attaining further possessions'. He recommended that the Earl of Ossory and his son, loyal to the crown, should take a number of castles, including 'Bon Raytte castle on the water of Limerick', and occupy Clare.

Bunratty, though an O'Brien stronghold, was not yet their chief seat and was apparently a matter of family dispute. On 11 March 1549 an agreement between the Earls of Thomond and Desmond was witnessed at Limerick by Sir William Brabazon, Lord Justice of Ireland, under which 'The Lord of Ybracan [the barony of Ibrackan, County Clare] and others are appointed arbitrators to settle the dispute between Sir Donell O'Bryan and his brother Sir Tirrelaghe about the division of the lands in Thomond as bretheren according to the custom of their country for the which Bunratye in the possession of the said Tirrelaghe is now in contention.' It was a time of great unrest. In 1553 Donough, the second Earl of Thomond and the English nominee, was replaced by his half-brother Donald, who was proclaimed O'Brien under the old Gaelic order. But he was in his turn replaced, with the aid of the English, by his nephew Conor who became the third earl in 1558. On 21 January 1560 Bunratty, together with several other Thomond castles, was granted to him under the instructions of Queen Elizabeth in consideration of his faithful services 'to hold in tail male by service of one knight's fee'.

In April 1570 Sir Edward Fitton was made president of Connacht, with which Thomond had been officially incorporated the previous year. He held the first assizes in Ennis Friary in what was, fifteen years later, to be officially shired as County Clare, thus usurping one of the remaining ancient privileges of the O'Briens. His reception by Conor was, however, so hostile that he abandoned the attempt after two days and retired to Galway. Sir Henry Sidney, the Lord Deputy, who described the Earl of Thomond as having 'neither wit of himself to govern, nor grace or capacity to learn from others', called upon James Butler, tenth Earl of Ormond – and Conor's cousin – to bring him to heel.

Ormond complained to Sidney from Limerick that the mayor had failed to co-operate and neglected to supply him with the boats necessary to approach Bunratty downriver, and he was obliged to attain his destination by land from Sixmilebridge through what was known as 'the long pass'. Conor, however, quickly submitted, asking to be allowed to go to England to plead his cause, and Ormond took possession of the castle in the queen's name, cutting more passes through the woods surrounding it in case hostilities would have to be resumed. On 4 June Ormond wrote to the Lord Deputy from Carrick-on-Suir that the Earl of Thomond had been proclaimed a rebel and had taken to the seas. He took refuge briefly in Paris, but by the beginning of December his rebellion, such as it was, was at an end. On 21st of that month he surrendered his land and his castles – both in Thomond and the county of Dublin – to the queen.

This development, which might appear as presaging the end of O'Brien hegemony, was, in effect, a recognised process within the political system of 'surrender and regrant' then obtaining, whereby the traditional lands and residences of the great native chiefs were confiscated and reassigned in exchange for firm professions of loyalty to the crown – professions which in many cases were dictated by expediency rather than conviction. Thus the O'Brien properties in County Clare were restored to them in 1573 with the provision that they would be forfeit in the event of further rebellion. Bunratty itself, at this period, would appear to have reverted very largely to a military role. A survey of Connacht and Thomond undertaken in 1574 by Sir Thomas Cusake and others listed – erroneously – 'the names of certain castles and towns within the County of Clare that were builded and erected by Englishmen – Inshiquyn and O'Brien's Bridge, Inysh and Qwynhy [Ennis and Quin], Clare and Bunratty', with the comment that 'in the old time these were good market towns and had English jurisdiction in them, and were governed by portriffes and other officers by authority of the King of England; but now they are all wasted and destroyed in a manner, saving the castles, and no part of the town walls left but old houses of stone work, broken gates and ruined walls.'

The 1570s marked a new era in the perennial Anglo-Irish conflict, characterised by a level of barbarity previously unknown even at the height of the Norman conquest: Henry VIII's 'sober waies' were submerged in a rising tide of sectarian bitterness and an attitude to the native Irish on the part of the new Elizabethan adventurers which barely accorded them human status. A key policy of the former and more enlightened approach had been one of social, cultural and political indoctrination: Donough O'Brien, who succeeded Conor as fourth Earl of Thomond in 1581, had been taken as a young man to England and educated in accordance with English manners and customs. 'He was one of those princelings that Elizabeth took over to her court,' said Marcus Ó hEochaidh. 'She had one of the De Burgos and Shane O'Neill, and these were later to be sent back as governors of their own provinces. In fact all three of them were to meet again at the battle of Kinsale [24 December 1601] – two remained loyal, the other went native.'

Donough was still a young man when he returned to County Clare, and for some time offered little evidence of his genteel English upbringing, gaining a reputation for 'robbing and spoiling' his neighbours. By 1585, however, when he was admitted to the parliament of Lord Deputy Sir John Perrott, he had reformed and demonstrated his loyalty to his mentors. In 1588 he was admitted to the council of Connacht and Clare but nearly lost his life trying to retrieve two brass pieces from the wrecks of the Armada ships on the Clare coastline. In the 1590s he took part in campaigns against the rebel Ulster earls O'Neill and O'Donnell, his military activity culminating in his being a signatory to the peace terms with Don Juan de Aguila after the battle of Kinsale. By this time he had become one of the most detested men in County Clare, in the view of his contemporaries 'more English than Irish'. His violent anti-Catholic crusade of 1615 offered his critics little encouragement to modify this view.

Donough's decision, on his accession to the earldom, to move the family seat to Bunratty Castle had afforded him the opportunity to indulge in a practical realisation of some of the desiderata of the good life which he had come to appreciate abroad, in particular as expressed in his domestic living conditions. 'Considerable alterations took place early in the sixteenth century under the Great Earl,' wrote T. J. Westropp. The castle as built by the Macnamaras was designed to withstand attack – hence the massive walls and the narrow slit windows affording protection rather than illumination. The alterations which perhaps most affected the external appearance of the building involved the windows: 'Externally imitation shallow quoins, long and short, were made round the windows of the towers,' wrote Westropp. 'The shafts of the south window were replaced by woodwork – it originally had three trefoil-headed lights and cusped tracery. The side windows, with two trefoil-headed lights in each, were also modified.' The Great Earl also filled his windows with leaded stained glass and reconstructed the roof, employing for both purposes lead from his mines at Roscrea, County Tipperary. In his will dated 28 November 1617 he bequeathed 'all my glass and leade in my house at Bunratty, being not set up in the wyndowes there, towards the glazing of the Cathedral Church of Limerick' with the exception of 'as much glass as will glaze the wyndowes of the church of Bunratty newly edified by me'.

The use of the word 'house' is significant: the earl's main purpose was to make a comfortable and fashionable dwelling in the English manner out of what had stood essentially as a fortified tower. When the art critic of *The Irish Times* visited the castle in May 1960 after the completion of its restoration, he noted 'One peculiarly English feature: the "solar" or private apartment for the Lord and his family... odd because English influence was at a low ebb.' If this were true in general, the earl's modifications clearly reflected his early influences – and his status as *Capitaneus Nationis Suae* – not only an earl under the English dispensation but, more importantly both in his own eyes and those of the O'Brien blood, chief of his name.

'It is difficult to realise to what a great extent ceremony and the dignity of estate formed the pattern of life among the nobly born,' wrote John Hunt, the major contributor to the antiquarian dimension of the castle's restoration. 'No one sat in his presence, except at dinner. His was the only chair in his Hall. In his

"Chair of Estate" he meted out justice, decided quarrels and received rents and tithes from his tenants and followers.' Thus Donough's sucessor, Henry, the fifth earl, under a lease granted on 20 January 1629 to Richard Keatinge of Ballynacraggia, County Clare, gentleman, required him to pay his rent of 13s. 4d. yearly 'in the hall of the manshion house of Bunratty with 2 hogs, 3 muttons and two capons at seasonable times towards the provisions of his house'.

'It was an aristocratic culture,' in the view of historian R. F. Foster, 'where the lowborn were of little account, and where a chief's authority was sustained by a complex, archaic and variable system of levies and taxation in kind, which presented yet another obstacle to the imposition of English systems.'

'Even a petty chief or nobleman,' John Hunt suggested, 'would have scores of attendants, stewards, retainers and followers, while in the castle of a great Prince, these would be increased to hundreds. Marshals, stewards, cooks, scullions, pages, footboys, grooms, herdsmen, huntsmen and a score of other callings would be constantly entering and leaving Bunratty Castle on their multifarious businesses... . Many of the Earl's followers would have lived in the now vanished town outside the Castle gates, but his lesser servants were housed in the clustering wooden huts and bothies within the Castle bawn and immediately outside the door. The earl and his family occupied the topmost and, therefore, safest rooms, and slept in beds, while his personal servants and officials would lie at night in the various small chambers, on truckle beds and straw paliasses, or huddled on the floors of the Great Hall and Main Guard.'

This view led Hunt to conclude that the upper rooms in the southern towers were contemporary with the fourth earl, as was the brick vaulting which crowned all four towers. This latter was substantially removed during restoration, ostensibly on the grounds of its instability but more significantly because it intruded upon Percy Le Clerc's master plan. The same fate attended a platform carried on heavy brick vaulting on the east side, adjoining the quay which lay between the castle and the river, as well as another part of the Great Earl's additions, a heavy brick vault between the two northern towers, designed to increase the living space. That the scholarly antiquarian in Hunt did not entirely welcome this rigorous reduction is suggested by his comment, in the booklet he wrote on the restored castle in 1964: 'All the buildings in brick have now been swept away and the castle stands as it did in the 15th century. Only certain additions of the 16th century at the top of the four towers and the plaster decorations in some of the rooms remain to show the Elizabethan alterations made at the time of the accession of the Great Earl in the late days of Elizabeth.' He might have added (though some would almost certainly have been of an earlier date) the sixteen garderobes or lavatories, an ample provision even for a castle of this size, and the room with a sloping floor and drainage aperture traditionally if controversially known as 'the earl's bathroom'.

Donough's new ideas extended beyond his castle walls. Formal gardens, in the Irish context, had not yet come to be regarded as necessary adjuncts to gracious country living. However, when Cardinal Rinuccini, the Papal Nuncio, visited Bunratty in 1646 at the height of the seige, he was so impressed with the setting that he wrote in a letter to his brother in Rome: 'Bunratty is the most beautiful place I have ever seen. In Italy there is nothing like the palace and grounds of Lord Thomond with its ponds and parks and its three thousand head of deer' – a view that might be considered as exalted by the enthusiasm of the moment had it not been echoed in very similar terms by his secretary Massari.

T. J. Westropp was mildly sceptical: 'It is hard to realise the rapturous account of Rinuccini as to this palace,' he wrote in the *North Munster Archaeological Journal* in 1915; 'he, too, to whom the magnificent fabrics of Italy and probably of other southern nations were familiar.' Be that as it may, the opinions of the cardinal and his secretary could not meaningfully be examined until, following the opening of the restored castle and folk park to visitors, it was found necessary in 1964 to provide a new entrance to the latter in an area to the west of the castle. At the request of Shannon Development, the Office of Public Works undertook an excavation on the site.

'The question of constructing a bawn wall with an entrance gateway arose,' said Marcus Ó hEochaidh, 'and it was with a view to discovering if any remains as such existed that I was brought in.' He uncovered the foundation course or footings of an original 17th century bawn wall; a second and earlier one was later identified. As work on building the new wall on the course of the old continued, a contractor was employed to begin work on the new entrance to the Folk Park. 'The minute he excavated his foundation trenches he ran into difficulties,' said Ó hEochaidh. 'A peculiar structure was discovered and they didn't know what it was. So work had to stop and I had to come back again and this led to the discovery of the Rinuccini Gardens and the moat.'

The gardens had been laid out on top of what had been the defensive moat – a trench cut across the promontory of glacial soil on which the castle stands. The excavation revealed two paved gardens, sloping down to the river. 'Some of the stonework,' said Ó hEochaidh, 'is reminiscent of the paving in the Great Hall. Some stones were probably rejects – the carving and the dressing is much fresher.' Quite apart from the significance of the gardens in confirming the extent of the Great Earl's improvement, they were very important, in Ó hEochaidh's view, 'because they seal the early mediaeval content of the moat – a very important archaeological deposit. The excavation did not proceed below the paving.' There were, however, some finds of minor importance: 'Nothing very spectacular,' Ó hEochaidh remembered, 'most of them domestic – very little association with war. They were an indication of the standard of living of the house. There was a nice collection of bellarmines [glazed drinking jugs with a capacious belly and narrow neck].'

'He found bits and pieces of coins and glass, tiles... a goblet,' recalled Christopher Lynch, who was closely involved with the restoration and became manager of the castle and Folk Park. 'Indeed, we were able to reproduce the original goblet for the castle banquets from evidence that was found in the excavation.'

There were other discoveries, including a mysterious tunnel under the road – 'It doesn't seem to lend itself to any explanation,' Le Clerc concluded. Another tunnel, which had been in use in recent years, was partially excavated in 1989 in connection with new Folk Park developments. The presence of vaulting in red brick suggested a further link with the improvements of the fourth earl. 'There was also the body – I should say the skeleton – of a female found in one of the moats,' Lynch recalled. 'I remember seeing it at the time. Marcus [Ó hEochaidh] had exposed it and we had brought out the local doctor to have a look, and he was able to tell us it was the body of a female teenager who died in childbirth. But it was left in situ and covered over after the excavation was over. And never mentioned actually because I think we didn't want to raise a hue and cry about it at the time.'

'O'Brien considered himself a proper English gentleman because when he came home he transformed his old mediaeval castle into an Elizabethan house with its gardens,' concluded Ó hEochaidh. In spite of his desire for elegance, it is scarcely likely that the earl's establishment and its tenantry could have stood

*Aerial view of the arch uniting the southern towers of Bunratty with the excavation of the Rinuccini gardens in progress*

aloof from the bloody strife involving other members of the O'Brien clan that marked the final decades of the 16th century, and which was to culminate in the great insurrection of 1641. In 1582 a namesake, Donough O'Brien, Lord Inchiquin, was hanged for treason at Limerick. In 1598 a letter from the same city to the Earl of Ormond provided an account of the military situation in the area, and it involved a close relative, the earl's brother Teig O'Brien. 'He maketh himself as strong as he can, and taketh all the castles he can in Thomond. The powder and furniture [stores] brought by Lowe into Thomond, under colour to land it in Bunratty, doth greatly further their traitorous purpose.' The earl, however, remained steadfast in his loyalty to the crown and duly reaped the rewards. He was appointed governor of Clare on 15 August 1599 and the following year entertained at Bunratty the Lord President of Munster, Sir George Carew, whom he was to succeed in office on 6 May 1615. He was confirmed in his holdings of lands under the crown by King James I in 1617 and died on 5 May 1624, succeeded by his son Henry. On 6 March 1627 a letter from the new king, Charles I, confirmed Henry 'in all his lands in Bunratty and Clonroad which had been previously held by his predecessor, Donough Earl of Thomond, deceased'.

The year 1633 saw the publication of a book with the lengthy and triumphalist title *Pacata Hibernia: Ireland Appeased and Reduced, or an Historie of the Late Warres in Ireland, especially within the Province of Munster under the Government of Sir George Carew*; but Ireland was far from being appeased and reduced. As England drifted towards civil war, the Ulster chiefs Hugh Óg MacMahon and Sir Phelim O'Neill planned rebellion. On 1 November 1641 Robert Coppinger, agent for Barnaby, Earl of Thomond, who had succeeded his elder brother Henry, was attending the fair at Clarecastle, County Clare, when news was brought to him from Limerick that the insurrection was in full swing. 'The rebels in Ireland pretended a commission from the King for what they did,' Edmund Ludlow wrote in his *Memoirs*, 'which so alarm'd the People of England, that the King thought himself necessitated to do something therein.' He said that when an army was raised he himself would lead it; but Parliament, suspecting the royal motives, decreed otherwise and itself raised a force of Scots and English troops.

On 31 August 1642 the Earl of Thomond wrote a plaintive letter[2] to the Commissioners of Irish Affairs with an account of 'those things that have happened since His Majesty's castle of Limerick being then taken by the rebels, and they thereby much strengthened and animated to wickedness'. He complained that the captain constable had deserted his post, leaving the river Shannon 'naked absolutely at the command of the rebels who, watchful to make use of so good an opportunity, brought a demi-cannon by water in boats, and thereby made themselves master of Askeaton and all the castles and holds that were invested by the English in the county of Limerick...'. And worse, he predicted, was to come – at least from his point of view: 'And the rebels being hereby much enabled are preparing the like attempt against the few castles I hold in this county, which I am no way able to oppose... . The city of Limerick, being not above six miles from [my] house, is so strong both by nature and art as I am confident the rebels have not a safer hold in Ireland, and till they be thence expelled there will never be quietness in these parts.' He further complained that the failure of their Lordships to come to his aid (his previous requests had apparently fallen on deaf ears) 'puts me in such despair as I account myself and all the English quite lost, whereas if I had in any convenient time but 1,000 men I could have been able to have made good all the castles near me and much quailed the strength of the enemy'.

Thomond did not get his thousand men or secure all his castles, but some help was nevertheless on the way. On 7 August the Scots and English force had arrived in Ireland in a fleet fitted out by London adventurers. Soon after their arrival, 'The Lord Forbes, a Scots-man, was sent with a party into Munster,' wrote Ludlow, 'where he greatly annoyed the enemy; and being furnished with some ships, sailed up the Shannon and secured several places upon that river, particularly Bonratte, the residence of the Earl of Thomond, where he found about threescore horse fit for service. Major Adams [McAdam] was made Governour of that House: But the Enemy frequently resorting to a Place called Six-Miles-Bridge, about two or three Miles from thence, the English pressed the Earl to assist them to fall upon the Irish; who unwilling to oppose the English Interest, and no less to make the Rebels his Enemies, endeavoured to excuse himself; yet upon second thoughts resolved to comply, if some care might be taken to spare his Kindred.'

In the long and bitter struggle that followed between the Confederates – an uneasy alliance of the Irish and the Catholic Old English – the Royalists and the Parliamentarians, the O'Briens were once more found with divided and wavering allegiances. Murrough O'Brien, sixth baron Inchiquin – the infamous 'Murchadh na dTóiteán', or 'Murrough of the Burnings' – abandoned the Royalist cause for that of the Parliamentarians on being refused the presidency of Munster in 1643. In December 1645 he met Adam Moulton in Bristol to explore the possibility of obtaining assistance from the English in gaining control of the port of Limerick and consolidating the power of the Parliamentarians in the mid-west. His cousin Barnaby, he told Moulton, was trying to remain neutral, but his tenants at Bunratty were already under instructions from the Confederates to withhold their rent and, in his cousin's view, the sixth earl of Thomond was prepared to see the Parliamentary cause in a more favourable light.

In this Inchiquin was no doubt simplifying the matter for the benefit of his listener. It was said of Barnaby, with little exaggeration, that he was 'Royalist, Rebel and Roundhead all at one and the same time'. At the Ennis sessions of 1642 he had obliged all those present to take an oath of allegiance to the king; his own loyalty, however, was to prove something less than consistent. On 12 August of the same year he had complained that the taking of Limerick Castle and other holdings of the English in County Limerick had left his own castles and lands open to attack from the 'Irish rebels' – the very people whom, as chief of the O'Briens, he was bound to protect.

Adam Moulton, nevertheless, was apparently convinced by Inchiquin as to the feasibility of the enterprise and the malleability of the Earl of Thomond and sailed from Bristol on 24 January

1646, reaching Cork three days later and conferring there with William Penn and Lord Broghill, vice-president of Munster, on the planning of the operation. Penn, still only 26, was in command of the *Fellowship* of the Irish squadron, in which he was to serve until 1650, rising to the rank of Vice-Admiral of the Irish Seas. Penn had a local connection: his wife Margaret, daughter of John Jasper, a Dutchman, had been born in the barony of Bunratty. Their son, William, was to become the founder of the American state of Pennsylvania; but the legend that as a young boy he was present with his father at the siege of Bunratty is, alas, no more than a legend. Even had naval regulations permitted, it is very unlikely that Penn senior would have introduced an infant of some 18 months into such an uncertain and perilous undertaking.

The naval force in which Penn served was under the control of the English parliament, and in the course of this service he was to form a close friendship with Inchiquin who was now, of course, supporting the same cause. The assembled squadron proceeded from Cork to Kinsale and from there to the Shannon,

*Barnaby O'Brien,
sixth Earl of Thomond*

where it anchored off Glin on the Limerick shore. On 11 March 1646, 'I received order from my admiral to take charge of all the frigates in the fleet,' Penn wrote in his journal, 'and to dispose of all the soldiers and seamen. About 3 in the afternoon I, being on board the *Peter* frigate, caused her to weigh, as also Capt. Browne, Capt. Swymmer, Capt. Liston, Capt. Farmer, Capt. Hall, and the hoy [a small sloop] to go up with me to Bonratty... . Between 6 and 7 we anchored near Bonratty, and sent a trumpeter to my Lord of Thomond, with a letter from my admiral and Lieut-Col. McAdam, who received it kindly, embracing our motion, and promising to join with us; but not being well himself, would send a gentleman of his to treat in his behalf.'

Barnaby's diplomatic illness set the pattern for what was to come. The following day Penn wrote to naval headquarters in England: 'We treated with the Earl concerning the cause of our coming, and desired his best assistance. We found him willing to further us in any thing, but fearful to hazard his person, and therefore was earnest for conveyance to England.' As well as having a natural desire to save his own skin, Barnaby was concerned to preserve his property and avoid the confiscations that inevitably attended those found on the wrong side at the wrong time. He had already yielded to Parliament in 1642; in 1645 he was 'advised' to seek reconcilation with his cousin Inchiquin by giving up Bunratty to him, advice he found it prudent to follow. Now, however, having handed over possession to Lieutenant-Colonel McAdam and Penn, he found himself under siege from the Confederate armies commanded by his step-nephew, Donough MacCarthy, Earl of Muskerry, who had acted as mediator between himself and Inchiquin. It is perhaps not surprising, in the circumstances, that he wanted out.

'Muskerry will not batter the house, his uncle's chief mansion place,' a contemporary historian wrote, 'alledging it to be a world of pittie to batter such a brave place'. Another contemporary described the castle in 1646 as 'a noble antient structure reputed strong when engines of battery were not so frequent... on the south of it, it has the river Shannon, distant from it about a mile, of marsh and meadow land. On the east it is washed with the river – [apparently the writer, the historian Richard Bellings, could not recall the name of the Owenogarney] which falling to the Shannon at the end of a goodly plain, ebbs and flows with it. To the north at some distance from the castle it is environed with an eminent ridge of earth, which bounds a goodly park; save that it wanted the ornament of timber trees, it was then stored with the largest deer in the kingdom. And to the west, the spacious plain of which we have previously spoken, was bounded with a broad deep trench... the receptacle of waters which issued from the springs in the neighbouring banks, and the waterish grounds that surrounded it. The space between the castle and the brow of the bank, which the garden took up, as being the most approachable, was well fortified with earthworks, and a mount raised wherein they planted 4 pieces of cannon. At some distance from this platform stood a little castle, and behind that the church on a rising ground, all within a deep trench, well flanked into which they intended to have drawn water from the river.'

Such were the preparations to withstand a siege by an army of 3,000 foot and some 300 horse, an army which had received no pay and no winter clothing and in which discontent was rife until Muskerry assumed command. 'The Lord of Muskerry having by his presence appeased the manie discontents of his souldiers and officers of the Mounster list,' wrote Bellings, 'and composed them to a body, being now furnished with some money, and his strength encreased by the access of the auxilaryes of Leinster, advanced to encamp in the parke of Bunratty, having taken a castle upon the quarter.. Here the soldiers, for some days, were refreshed with plenty of venizon...'. Marcus Ó hEochaidh suggested that it was at this time that the bawn walls which he excavated had been thrown down to give the English cavalry an open field of fire to ride down the ridge towards where the Confederates were encamped.

On 22 March all old men, women and children were evacuated from Bunratty town by Penn's vessels. The following day he sent carpenters ashore to build a platform on a half-allowance 'by reason of the scarcity of our provisions'. The men not unnaturally objected, demanding meat instead of the extra pay offered in lieu. The work proceeded, and on the 31st Penn went ashore himself to inspect it and 'to take order with the lieutenant-colonel for the raising and flooring of the mount in the garden'. On 1 April a Confederate raiding party set fire to seven houses in Bunratty town and, as Penn laconically noted in his journal, 'killed some English etc'. A retaliatory attack on the Irish camp yielded a prize of 250 barrels of oatmeal 'which served the soldiers 6 weeks for bread, our supplies being much exhausted'. Though Penn held undisputed command of the Shannon, his garrison of some 700 in Bunratty was continuously short of essential supplies.

On 9 April the garrison was strengthened by 'pulling down walls, removing thatched houses out of the town into a field adjoining the castle'. Penn gave orders for 'the making of a platform for a great gun in the pigeon-house'. On the 28th some of his men deserted to the enemy, or the 'rogues' as he invariably described them: a letter written from the Confederate headquarters at Kilkenny at this time announced that 'the greatest news here is the siege of Bunrathe from whence some English and Welsh soldiers that love our king stole away'. (The Confederates, though seeking an independent Irish parliament, nevertheless recognised the English monarchy.)

At Bunratty the siege appeared close to stalemate. 'Now although much time was spent,' wrote Bellings, 'yet the besiegers found that they had done little more to the carrying of the castle, and the mastering of the enemy's works, than to have lodged themselves in the neighbourhood; for they not only had the sea open to them, but they were supplied with fresh meat, and forage for their horses from that large piece of pasture ground which lay between the castle and the river of the Shannon.' Barnaby, however, judged that the time had come to undetake a strategic withdrawal and leave the combatants to their own devices. On 8 May 'the Earl of Thomond's goods came down in boats on board of [Capt.] Grigge', wrote Penn. The next day he recorded that 'Near upon eight in the morning, the Earl of Thomond came down from Bunratty and went on board Capt.

Grigg to go for Cork; I went on board to wait upon his honour....
About 2, my Lord of Thomond came on board our ship to dinner; I gave his lordship 5 guns at his entering.' On 10 May Penn
went on board Captain Grigg's ship to dine again with Barnaby,
and the following morning about ten 'Capt. Grigge weighed for
Cork... . I went down with my lord on Grigg's ship as far as the
Glen [Glin], where I took leave of his honour.'

Thus departed, with scant ceremony and little honour, the last
of the Earls of Thomond to occupy the castle of Bunratty.

### Notes

[1] Thomas O'Gorman (1732-1809) was a Clareman who qualified as a doctor at
the Irish College in Paris, became a close friend of King Louis XV and in the
course of his frequent return visits to Ireland collected many valuable manuscript
sources for Irish history.

[2] Spelling modernised.

# The End and the Beginning

I T WAS NOT exactly a voyage into the unknown, still less the bitter path of exile. This wild goose had long since had his wings clipped, and, a West Briton three centuries before the label gained currency, was retreating not to loneliness and poverty in a foreign land but to the country he most probably thought of as his true home. For this, his early upbringing apart, he had sound practical reason, being the possessor through the favour of the English of a substantial estate and a minor title to go with it. He was to spend the rest of his days at the manor of Great Billing in Northamptonshire and to be buried there. He had already shed his given name, Brian, in favour of the distinctively non-Irish Barnabas – though he must have been more than a little irritated when his compatriots naturalised it to Barnaby – and now he proceeded to dispose of the last badge of identity. *Níl Mac ná Ó aige*, he became plain Barnaby Brien. A generation later his grandson Henry was to exemplify the effective meaning of that Irish phrase: 'He had no one to succeed to his name.' With the death of Henry Brien the line of the Earls of Thomond became extinct.

Great Billing did not, however, absorb Barnaby without trace. Before long he was petitioning the English parliament for compensation for the wrongs he claimed to have suffered in their cause. He asserted 'his own innated abhorring of the rebellion of the Irish, even from the very first rise of it, and this, in all times since, he has manifested to the world... nor hath he continued at Bunratty out of any other end than by his personal abode there to preserve it from the Irish, and keep it ready for the Protestant English and Parliament'. He calculated his 'sufferings by rebellion' at £42,173 13s. 4d., which included £35,000 'taken by the Irish rebells' and £5,000 'in stock of cattle, beasts and sheepe'. The goods 'left in the castle att his Lordship's coming away' included 'a barrel of sherry att £2; two hogsheads white wine att £8; 9 hogsheads of stronge beere at 10s [per hogshead]; 30 hogsheads of ordinary beere at 9s; 400 weight of candle 33s 4d', as well as barley, wheat, malt and oats.

This, however, was by no means the full extent of his alleged losses. On 2 July William Penn, visiting the castle, 'found some of the officers in McAdam's chamber, having there 18 bags of money, and some plate, before them which, with two more formerly disposed of, were found by the lieutenant-colonel in the castle. I perceiving them to be resolute in sharing the money among them, willed them to consider that money is the nerves and sinews of war... . But what power my poor rhetoric to this purpose had you may guess... .'

Edmund Ludow's account put a somewhat different interpretation on the event. Thomond, he wrote, when invited by the Parliamentarians to offer some firm evidence of his support for their cause, 'chose rather to withdraw himself into England, and to leave his House to the Souldiers, where (tho he pretended he had no Money to lend them to supply their wants) they found two thousand Pounds buried in the Walls, which they made use of for the paiment of their Forces'.

Ludlow's account was borne out by the attestation of Sir Arthur Loftus 'touching the Earle of Thomond's £2400' and certified under his hand on 2 November 1646. He stated that 'I Sir Arthur Loftus, Colonell of the regiment lately at Bunratty in the Kingdome of Ireland, have received severall informacions of accounts by letters from my officers of the truth of what my Lo: of Thomond setts forth to the committee of Lords and Commons for Irish affaires; and by those letters I am confirmed that there was £2400 of his Lordship's mony made use of in paying 3 monetghes pay to every officer and reformado in the regioment, and sent from Munster and raised there for deefence of the place in ramsomeing the souldiers, being between 4 and 500 men, by laying downe for every one a monethes pay or thereabouts.' The parliamentary committee in London appointed to adjudge Thomond's claims was sympathetic, though not all that sympathetic. They reduced the demand to £2,400; perhaps significantly close to the amount that had disappeared from its mural hiding place. It was still a substantial sum, but a long way short of what the fugitive earl had hoped for.

Meanwhile the situation at Bunratty, from the English point of view, continued to deteriorate. Penn had sent back several of Barnaby's household who had hoped to escape with him, but on 20 May he had been obliged to evacuate more women and children, 'necessity forcing their departure in a greater number than could be imagined'. The outposts occupied by the Parliament-arians were falling: a week previously the Irish forces had attacked one of them, Cappagh Castle, and 'having entered the castle and taken our men prisoners, they marched from thence to a castle called Rossmonnahane, not a full mile from Bunratty, formerly commanded by one Hunt; which, but two days before, he quit, and was now with his wife and family in Bunratty castle', where three hundred years later another Hunt was to take up residence in somewhat less threatened circumstances.

On 14 May Penn spent the morning at the fortifications which were being installed on the rectangular mound, anxious to see the work completed in preparation for what he judged to be an imminent attack. The Irish had advanced and set fire to some of the houses on the nearby hill, provoking retaliation from the gar-rison who marched out and 'fired some of the Irish cabins'. The attack came on the 18th but was thrown back. There was another on the 29th, and the next day Muskerry, now encamped in front of the castle, sent letters to McAdam. Whether these contained an invitation to surrender or the offer of negotiations is not apparent, but the garrison were finding it more and more diffi-cult to sustain themselves. On 4 June they had to move their cows to the relative security of a nearby island, but lost to the enemy 'about 80 mares and colts, being feeding over in the mar-ishes'. Nor were shipboard conditions in Penn's vessels very much easier. On 19 June he wrote that 'we not having 16 days' beer for the state ships now in this squadron, it was conceived necessary that our empty casks should be sent to Kinsale, there to be fitted and filled with beer, and so returned to us by the next conveyance'. With adequate water always difficult to procure, these were considered essential supplies.

At Westminster the Committee of both Houses for Irish Affairs was concerned at the way things were going. On 17 June it resolved that the Earl of Thomond put in writing his scheme for reinforcing Bunratty – apparently his departure had not yet been officially recognised – and that 500 men be raised for the purpose, 'An estimate to be made of the charge for 3 months victual for the garrison (in all 1,200 men) and of a full equipment of ammunition and siege implements for these.' But it was a little late in the day. On 28 June McAdam asked Penn for all the men and arms he could possibly spare since he had received word that the garrison was about to be stormed. On 1 July the Papal Nuncio, Cardinal Rinuccini, arrived in the Irish camp. Lodged in 'a hovel built of earth and covered with straw', his presence immeasurably strengthened the morale of the Confederates, and he urged an immediate attack. The same day Penn was dining with McAdam in the castle, 'at which, the lieutenant-colonel sitting, the rebels made divers shots at Jefford's House, which they had often attempted to gain, but as yet could not. He (hearing them shoot so thick, and ply their guns so hard) rose from the table, went to the house to see what breaches were made, and to encourage his men; where being entered, a shot was made, by which the lieutenant-colonel, John McAdam, was most unhappily slain, to the general lamentation of us all.' He 'received a shot about his hams from a field-piece that was planted among the gabions [wicker baskets filled with earth used for fortifications],' wrote Bellings, 'and being carried thence, dyed that night.'

It was a blow from which the Parliamentarians were not to recover. On 3 July Penn sent Captain Clarke aboard the frigate *Charles* to Kinsale to seek urgent assistance from Lord Broghill. 'I sent one of our boats up, with provisions for our men, at whose return I was informed... that another Welchman, running away the last night, told the enemy of the death of the lieutenant-colonel; who called to our men, and bid them "get a better commander"... I would such rogues might be hanged, for example's sake.' Things went from bad to worse. The following day there was another desertion: 'A Frenchman, a trooper of ours, ran away to the rogues, with his horse, pistols and carbine. The enemy got a gun down this day into the corcasse, which flanks all our works, and will thereby do us much damage.' (This was the marshy area – from the Irish *corcach*, a marsh – on the western side of the castle.) It was completely under Confederate control by the 10th, and the following day they also occupied the corcasse to the east, cutting off the supply route to Bunratty by water.

A major – whom Penn does not name and for whom he obviously had scant respect – had taken over the command on the death of McAdam. On 11 July this officer told Penn that 'the soldiers were so much wasted with over duty, so much discouraged by the loss of the corkasse, and so much overpowered by the enemy's multitudes, that they would not stand any longer to their arms'. They hoped to negotiate an honourable surrender with Muskerry allowing them to march out of Bunratty with drums beating and colours flying and so overland to Cork, but these terms were flatly rejected and, in Belling's words, 'they were content to capitulate for their lives only, and the officers their swords, leaving the place, cannon, horses, ammunition, and provisions to the Confederates, and, embarqueing their sick and wounded men, returned by sea to Cork'.

Penn's disgust was that of the naval disiplinarian for a landsman whom he clearly believed had failed in his military duty and shown a culpable lack of resolution in the face of the enemy. 'About seven this morning [14 July] came down a boat from the rebels, with a captain of theirs, a lieutenant and ensign of ours, with certain articles of agreement (interchangeably signed, by the Lord Muskerry on their part and the major and officers on ours) for the surrender of the castle. The conditions were so mean, and so far beneath the honour of a soldier, that I should never have consented thereunto. Yet things past cure ought to be past care... . About nine the hoy, with all our boats, returned from Bunratty, as full of soldiers and inhabitants, men, women and children, as they could thrust, which put me to no small trouble to dispose of... .' The next morning the remainder of the inhabitants with their commanders came down river, 'having quit the garrison, and the rebels taken possession of it; which did not a little grieve me, after all the cares and pains I had taken, night and day'. On the way down the Shannon with his seriously overloaded vessels Penn was constrained, for want of a favourable wind, to put the former inhabitants of Bunratty ashore to wash and pick themselves clean of lice. Setting sail again he met the token relief force sent by Broghill from Kinsale: too little and too late.

In Westminster the deliberations of the Committee on Irish Affairs had also been overtaken by events. On the day after McAdam was shot, 2 July, they ordered that 'John Davies is to provide and send away to the castle of Bunratty in Co. Clare £1,200 worth of victual, 40 barrels of English powder, 2 1/2 tons of Bullet, 100 hand granadoes [grenades], 50 whole culverin shot, 150 minion shot, 60 shot for drakes [small cannon], £10 worth of sacks, scythes and hooks, £10 worth of spades, shovels, and pickaxes.' On the 8th they further ordered: 'John Davies shall also deliver to William Dobbins, gent., commissary for the provisions to be sent to Ireland, a syrgeon's chest, value £25, iron and steel value £20, smith's coals value £3, candlewick value £5, pistols, swords, etc., consigned to the Governor of Bunratty.' Dobbins was instructed to hire a ship to carry this impressive cargo of necessaries, but official wheels turned slowly. By 28 July the Committee was obliged to set up a sub-committee 'to expedite the sending away of the ship which is carrying arms and provisions to Bunratty'. On 13 August it ordered 'provisions to be sent at once to Cork for Bunratty'. Though a pass had been issued to one Ensign John Plummer on 23 September to make his way back to the castle, 'whence he had brought letters from Colonel McAdam, governor of that place', his dispatches had obviously left the Committee on Irish Affairs in ignorance as to the real nature of the situation.

If William Dobbins was unable to comply with his instructions, Lord Broghill's ill-fated relief expedition had at least set sail whilst there was still some hope of its proving effective. As late as 1654, however, Captain Giles Shelley, who had been offered £200 by Broghill to transport men and provisions from Cork to Bunratty in his ship *Dainty*, of London, was attempting to recoup his outlay on a mission doomed to failure. On his first attempt, he wrote in a petition to the Lord Protector, Oliver Cromwell, he had been driven back by contrary winds; on his second he had learnt in mid-voyage that Bunratty had fallen. He had received a letter to this effect from Lord Inchiquin informing him that 'the place you were to relieve is lost'. He had, he said, spent a month at this work for which he had received no payment. It was recommended he be recompensed in the sum of £60.

On 22 July the Committee had also dealt with a request, presumably contained in letters written before the Earl's departure on 9 May and brought by Ensign Plummer, that 'the commander at his house of Bunratty, Co. Clare, shall allow his lordship's servant Christopher Hart to embark and bring to Bunratty six useful horses for the use of his Lordship and of his sons, together with plate, writings, money, etc. for the Earl. His lordship is willing to receive Sir Arthur Loftus' regiment into his house, to furnish them with necessaries, and to fit out a troop of Reformadoes, all of his own horse for the Guard of Bunratty.' 'Yet now for the making good of soe important a place for the State's service as Bunratty is,' Thomond had written, 'and for the preservation of the forces already there, it is humbly desired that the forces of Munster may be made up 5000, and bee directed eyther by diversion or otherwise to remove the Irish now before it... and that the Lord Brien, heire and sole sonne to the Earle of Thomond, may alsoe have a regiment of foote and a troop of horse with assured pay assigned to him; and the horses and armes hee undertakes to provide wholly at his own charge (if those of his father's left at Bunratty may be delivered to him) with authority to command in cheife in that county as deputy to his father, who hath the government thereof fixed in him by patent during life... .' However, this plan to secure both Bunratty and the Thomond succession there had already succumbed to events.

As far as Bunratty was concerned the Confederates had won the battle; but as the Parliamentarians brought more powerful and ruthless forces to bear in the years that followed, and their opponents split into divisive political and religious factions, it was inevitable that they should lose the war. In 1647 their council observed that 'the enemy was so powerful in that province [Munster] as to have been able that summer both to regain what they had lost the year before, and to make such a diversion in Bunratty as for four months found work for the army designed for the service of Munster'. The following year Inchiquin marched into Limerick and some of his men crossed the Shannon at O'Brien's Bridge, whereupon the Irish burned Bunratty. It cannot on this occasion have amounted to a total destruction, since some four years later Edmund Ludlow was to recuperate from his hard campaigning in its hospitable surroundings; and on 8 September 1651 it was considered by the Parliamentary army command to be 'fit to be fortified' and was garrisoned by Captain Preston with a troop of horse and a foot company.

Oliver Cromwell had come and gone and left in his wake death and destruction. With Ireton dead, it fell to Edmund Ludlow to complete the conquest. On 21 April 1652 Colonel Murtagh O'Brien, commander of the Confederate forces in County Clare, surrendered to Sir Hardress Waller in Limerick. He himself succeeded in joining Donough MacCarthy, Lord Muskerry, for what was to be the Confederates' last stand at Ross Castle on the lower lake of Killarney. Ludlow took personal command of the campaign, and his stratagem of bringing boats to attack the fortress by water so dismayed the garrison (a local legend asserted that 'Ross may all assault disdain/Till strange ships sail on Lough Laune') that it capitulated on 22 June, marking the end of organised resistance in Munster. For the vanquished there was nothing to expect but execution or exile. As Daibhidh Uí Bhruadair, the Munster poet, wrote:

*Aon troigh amháin níor fágbhadh acu*
*mar dheire ón stát na ádhbhar leaptha,*
*dobhearaid grása daibh is aite*
*a leigion slán don Spáinn ar eachtaibh.*

A foot of land has not been left in their possession
Nor even the makings of a bed, as state-doled pittance
They will grant them now the favour and the pleasure
Of letting them go safe to Spain by proclamations.

By now Bunratty Castle had effectively played its last active role
in the turbulent history of its county and country. Of the count-
less men and women involved in its fortunes through the passage
of four centuries, the major actors have at best appeared in
cameo roles: de Clare, with his eye to the main chance; the Great
Earl with his foreign foibles a tacky veneer on his O'Brien heritage; Penn, the practical and impatient seaman fallen among
fools; and Edmund Ludlow, regicide and committed republican,
shivering in a damp bed in the Burren. HIC JACET EDMUND
LUDLOW, TUNC HYBERNORUM DOMITOR, IN PUGNA
INTREPIDUS, ET VITAE PRODIGUS, IN VICTORIA
CLEMENS boasts his Swiss memorial. If indeed he was – in addition to being full of fight and full of life – merciful in victory, his
total disdain for his Irish enemies offers little enough evidence.

As to the rest, the 'ordinary' men and women – particularly the
women – who lived all this time in and about Bunratty, history is
virtually silent. 'Ordinary people,' as the poet Louis MacNeice
observed, 'are peculiar too'; but the peculiarities of the burgers
of the Norman town, of the servants of the Great Earl, of
Barnaby's tenants who watched their cabins go up in smoke, can,
at this distance, only be guessed at.

And if this is true of the centuries in which Bunratty was in
time's eye, it is even more so of the long expanse of empty years
that were to follow. A succession of absentee Thomond land-
lords effectively undermined a social and political centrality
which, with the final collapse of the Gaelic order and the flight of
the Wild Geese, was in any case doomed to destruction. The

next Lords of Thomond to occupy the great chair in the great hall would be New World vacationers, earls for an evening.

For the moment, however, the sixth earl, though comfortably ensconced on his English estates, had by no means forfeited his interest in Bunratty. His affairs in Ireland were left in the hands of stewards who, in the absence of direct supervision, wielded considerable power. As one grasping and unscrupulous individual gave place to another, Barnaby seemed on each occasion to have chosen badly. Between 1650 and 1681 the Thomond interests were at the mercy of a succession of incompetents, if not outright villains, with the result that the estates became seriously neglected. Barnaby had, nevertheless, apparently remained in hope that the Earls of Thomond would one day reassume their inheritance. In March 1646, a year before his death, he leased 'Bunratty, one Quarter' to a John Cooper, to be surrendered on a year's warning 'if my Lord or his Sonne comes to settle here'.

This lessee may be identical with a 'Cornet Cooper' of the Cromwellian army whom Máire Rua O'Brien subsequently married as her third husband to save her estates: her second husband, Conor O'Brien, was killed by Ludlow's forces in 1650. Máire Rua, born about 1615 and the daughter of Torlach Rua MacMahon, lord of Clonderlaw, was the focus of an extraordinary body of legend and half-truths which passed into the folklore of the region. She was reputed to have gone through between twelve and twenty-five husbands, to have kept menservants dressed as women at her castle of Leamaneh, and to have subjected her succession of suitors to ordeal by stallion, obliging them to mount a beast which carried them to the Cliffs of Moher and unseated them to fall 200 metres to the rocks below.

The historical Máire was remarkable enough to explain the genesis of these legends. She certainly married three times, her first husband, Daniel Neylon, dying young and leaving her with four children. Within eight months she had married Conor O'Brien, master of Leamaneh, but the shadow of Cromwell was falling over Ireland. In 1651, as a royalist officer supporting the exiled King Charles II, O'Brien confronted a raiding party led by Edmund Ludlow and was mortally wounded. Máire was forced to leave Leamaneh, which was captured by Cromwell's forces, and in circumstances that are not clear called upon John Cooper to witness a will made by her seventeen-year old son as a means of protecting the family property. Tradition has it that Cooper, having married Máire about 1653, subsequently died either as a result of his being thrown by Máire over the battlements of Leamaneh, or more prosaically, as a result of a kick she gave him when he ventured to cast aspersions on her former husband, who retained first place in her affections.

Máire and Cooper did not, apparently, live at Bunratty, but an O'Brien presence persisted: a letter from one Colonel Daniel O'Brien dated 22 January 1669 states, 'I am with my Lord O'Brien [in County Galway] catching dear to stock the park at Bonrattie.' Another dated 3 May of the same year, from 'Mr O'Brien of Bunratty' to the same recipient, a Joseph Williamson, informs him that 'Lord O'Brien is making good use of his time in these parts. If he lives there will be none in this kingdom in a few years that will be better able to serve His Majesty [Charles II] with greater number of men than he.' The 'Lord O'Brien' referred to was presumably Baron O'Brien of another branch of the extended family.

Barnaby was succeeded as seventh Earl of Thomond by his son Henry, who showed no inclination to return to live in County Clare. In 1673, however, he was in partnership with a local merchant in the business of exporting hides and tallow through Limerick and Cork, an enterprise which no doubt suffered at the hands of the latest occupant of the steward's house at the castle, built in the precincts by the sixth earl and which had apparently survived the siege. In 1681 Thomas Spaight, who had then been six years in the earl's employ, succeeded to the office and prospered to the extent that his descendants were considered – or considered themselves – one of the leading families in the counties of Clare and Limerick: a James Spaight was mayor of Limerick city in 1856.

The castle – or at least the manor – continued for some time to function as an administrative centre: Courts Baron and Courts Leet (the latter a court of record held periodically before the lord or his steward) are mentioned in the records of the 1670s. In 1712 Henry, Earl of Thomond, the eighth and last of his line, leased some lands to Sir Donough O'Brien of Dromoland, with the proviso that 'lessee to pay a year's rent at renewal time, to do suit and service at the manor court of Bunratty and to maintain a protestant horseman for a month in attendance on Lord Thomond, if required'. The protestant horse was to remain in his stable. In 1599 Dromoland had been given by Murrough O'Brien to his third son Donough and became, after the sacking of Leamaneh castle by Cromwell, the residence of the Barons Inchiquin until it was sold in 1962.

In the same year – 1712 – that he leased lands to the Dromoland O'Briens, Henry sold the Bunratty estate to Thomas Amory for the sum of £225 and an annual rent of £150. It comprised 'The castle farm and lands of Bunratty of 472 acres' and the terms stipulated 'free ingress, egress and regress for coach or cart through the park of Bunratty to the town of Sixmilebridge', reserving to the earl 'all minerals, waifes, strayes, deodants [personal chattels], felons' and fugitives' goods, treasure trove, all advowsons and presentations of churches, vicarages, and seneschalships, and profits of Court Leete and Court Baron, with free liberty to hunt and hawke, fish and fowl, upon the premises, and all other Royalties whatever'. Presumably to facilitate the ingress, egress and regress, the road from Bunratty to Sixmilebridge was repaved in 1714.

On 26 November 1725 Thomas Amory sold an interest in the fee-farm grant to Thomas Studdert, then of Kilkishen, for £1,600 and a further sum as a mortgage. Henry, last Earl of Thomond, died without issue on 29 April 1741. The earldom, in passing from history, left one curious linguistic legacy. An entry in Captain Francis Grose's *Dictionary of the Vulgar Tongue* (1785) reads: 'THOMOND. Like Lord Thomond's cocks, all on one side. Lord Thomond's cock-feeder, an Irishman, being entrusted with some cocks which were matched for a considerable sum, the night before the battle shut them all together in one room, concluding that as they were all on the same side, they would not disagree: the consequence was, they were most of them killed or lamed before the morning.' A posthumous valediction to the family reputation for equivocal allegiances.

The Studderts were an Anglo-Irish family which had been settled in counties Clare and Limerick since 1699. They were to remain in possession of Bunratty for two hundred years, during which time the once-proud castle subsided slowly but steadily into anonymity and decay. The process was hastened when the family built itself a new residence – now known as Bunratty House – in the grounds at the same time as they bridged the river and ceased to use the castle itself as a principal dwelling. They also, however, built – according to a contemporary account – 'a commodious quay which is about to be enlarged. Boats of a large size can come up to it. Considerable quantities of sea manure and turf is brought here from Kilrush' – an indication that, in contrast to the castle itself, the village of Bunratty, which in the early 1800s had a population of some 1,300 and three schools, was prospering. The anchorage off Quay Island known as Bunratty Road continued to be of importance: it was used by West India vessels to discharge their cargoes for Limerick. Bunratty held regular fairs for cattle, pigs and sheep as well as the occasional seneschal's court dealing with local matters.

Meanwhile, in spite of its neglected condition, the castle continued to attract the attention of the curious and the romantic: 'This once celebrated castle, wrote the *Dublin Penny Journal* in December 1833, 'appears to have been a strong, square pile of massive architecture, and like many edifices of a similar kind, to have suffered much from various attacks of an enemy. In many places its walls have been deeply indented with cannon shot... several cannon balls have been found about it, one of which weighed thirty-nine pounds.' Five years later the peripatetic Lady Chatterton paid a visit which she recorded in her *Rambles in the South of Ireland*: 'Nearer to Shannon is Bunratty castle, a most interesting object, of which we stopped to make a sketch. It is in excellent preservation, and was inhabited, not long since, by the family to whom it belongs. A singular discovery was made in this castle, while it was thus tenanted. Some repairs being required in one of the apartments, workmen were employed, who, on removing part of the floor, discovered a vast chamber underneath. They descended into it, and found it hung with magnificent brocaded silk, a quantity of the same rich material being folded up, and lying on the ground, which, however, afterwards fell to pieces, on being exposed to the air. In the middle of the subterrranean apartment was a skeleton, with a long knife beside it, the handle of which was of massive silver, splendidly chased. The most extraordinary circumstance connected with the discovery was, that there was no apparent exit to the chamber: no trace of either door or window could be seen.'

There is, apparently, no other recorded witness to this strange sight; and perhaps it might be as well to recall that this was the age of the romantic imagination and the Gothic novel. Secret rooms, on the other hand, were a not uncommon feature of mediaeval architecture (a particularly impressive example was discovered during the excavations at St John's Castle, Limerick, in the early 1990s) and there was speculation as to similar features in Bunratty when restoration was undertaken. 'By doing a survey of the castle you can see where there might be a room,' said Percy Le Clerc, 'a room for instance in that wall down in the basement on the west side. The wall is fourteen feet thick.' He was not, however, convinced: 'Quite obviously it is quite possible that there might be some chamber inside that massive amount of masonry, but I doubt it.' A small room, was, however, discovered in the course of the work, but it had been walled off and forgotten about rather than originally constructed as a secret chamber.

The successors to the policeman who showed Thackeray over the castle in 1842 were still in occupation, as the Royal Irish Constabulary, when on 25 August 1914 Thomas Studdert wrote to the Commissioners of Public Works on the advice, as he said, of the Secretary of the Royal Society of Antiquaries of Ireland. Three weeks before, Great Britain had declared war on Germany; and only the outbreak of hostilities had prevented the coming into force of the Home Rule Bill which was to grant Ireland limited independence. It had been passed by Westminster against strong unionist opposition but was suspended for the duration on 18 September. In July a conference at Buckingham Palace had attempted without success to bring together the deeply divided unionist and nationalist factions, which had been running in arms to their respective paramilitary forces. On the 26th of the same month the yacht *Asgard*, navigated by Erskine Childers, eponymous father of the man who was to play a significant role in the restoration of Bunratty, had landed 1,500 guns for the Irish Volunteers at Howth, County Dublin.

It would seem on the face of it an inauspicious time to have been asking a public body to interest itself in the taking over of a large and ruinous castle, but Thomas Studdert could, no doubt, foresee even harder times ahead. 'The Police Barracks are now occupied by a station of the RIC who pay me a rent of £20 per annum,' he told the Commissioners. 'The Barracks is an addition to the castle, built on 100 or 200 years ago. There is an opening from the Barracks into two rooms of the old Castle, in occupation by the Police. If the Board took over the ruins, might I ask if any payment would be made in respect of alterations or improvements made during the past 20 or 30 years to the ruins?'

'The building is roofed and the walls are pretty sound,' an internal board memo noted on foot of Studdert's letter, 'and any portion of it that is of use to the RIC is occupied by them. The

*The castle from an early 20th century postcard*

rest is vacant. The owner is not willing to undertake the cost of keeping such a large building in repair, hence the application. He makes no mention of vesting it.' The memo suggests that if offered the castle should be considered for acquisition, but that a reply should make clear that no payment could be made in respect of work done by the owner.

There were two methods under which the Commissioners of Public Works in Ireland could take ancient monuments into their care: vesting and guardianship. The former involved the handing over of the property *in toto* with certain minor exclusions; the latter permitted the owner to retain a significant interest and to continue to live on the site. The relevant legislation applicable at this time in Ireland was embodied in the Ancient Monuments Protection Acts of 1882 and 1892 which stated, *inter alia*, that if requesting the Commissioners of Public Works in Ireland to become guardians an owner must appoint them by deed. Estate, right and title would still be held, except that the owner must undertake not to deface or otherwise damage the monument. 'The ancient Monument includes the site of such Monument, and such portion of land adjoining the same as may be required to fence, cover in, or otherwise preserve from injury, the Monument standing on such a site, also the means of access to such a Monument.' Studdert was undecided as to which of these two avenues to pursue, and on 20 January 1916 wrote again to the Commissioners asking if they would consider taking over Bunratty and if so under what conditions.

Public interest in the fate of the castle had been heightened during the previous year by the extensive contributions of George Macnamara and T. J. Westropp to the *North Munster Archaeological Journal* and the article, based on these, in *The Irish Builder*. 'We note that the owner, Mr Thomas Studdert, has generously offered to vest the Castle in the Board of Works,' the latter wrote. 'We hope that no time will be lost in availing of this offer... .' In June 1916 Bunratty was visited by members of the Royal Society of Antiquaries of Ireland who expressed the view that 'the whole is of great interest and should be vested as a National Monument'. The Commissioners had, however, already decided to respond to *The Irish Builder*'s appeal and to Studdert's latest letter, and on 28 January had sent their inspector, W. Salmond, to assess the physical status of the castle. On 18 February he reported that the main apartment on the ground floor (now generally referred to as the basement) was being used as a turf store and a portion under the eastern terrace as stables. The barracks had no connection with the main structure except that its chimney flues were built on or into the exterior walls. (In this, as it transpired, he was not altogether correct.) 'The castle walls are plumb and there are no dangerous cracks in same,' wrote Salmond, 'while there is practically no vegetation (and scarcely any ivy) except on vaulted roofs of turrets and on wall-heads; some pointing and general cleaning up is required; the wallheads, as far as can be seen, do not need any weathering. The turret roofs cannot be seen for grass &c. There is no roof over the main central portions... . Generally the premises are in very fair condition &, both from this point of view & from their historical interest, I think they are well worthy of most favourable consideration with a view to vesting in the Board.' A note to this report by Robert Cochrane, then the board's Inspector of National Monuments, observed that the castle did not appear to be fully offered for vesting and that the owner wished to retain an interest. It recommended that this matter should be cleared up.

The next move involved the production of plans to 1/8 inch scale, a task entrusted to H. G. Leask, a future Inspector of National Monuments who, though then a relatively junior employee of the board (which he had joined in 1909), had been elected president of the Architectural Association of Ireland in 1915. The plans showed that the prison cell of the RIC barracks, which rose to three storeys on the north-west side of the castle, was actually built into the thickness of the walls and that there was also access from the barracks to the south-western tower – from which, however, there was no passage to the castle proper. The cell itself, windowless and measuring no more than 40 inches by 112, must have seriously discouraged local wrongdoing. A further report dated 14 April 1916 made the point that there was no ground now attached to the property and suggested that 'If suitable terms can be agreed with Mr Studdert the Board ought certainly to accept the vesting in them of this, one of the most important castles in the south and west of Ireland. The vesting should be complete and there must be no difficulty in closing all means of access from the RIC to the castle in the SW tower. The ground floor of the castle will of course be given up by the Landlord in the event of this vesting proceeding... .' Studdert was to be asked if he wished to dispose of his interest in the barracks and if so on what terms.

The board wrote to Studdert to this effect on 9 May, stating that it would accept either guardianship or vesting but would prefer the latter. Studdert replied that 'It would certainly be a matter of public interest that the castle should be properly preserved, and I would do everything possible to enable this to be done. At the same time, there are certain considerations affecting the control of the key, whereby the interests of the local residents would clash with those of the local publican, and I should be obliged if you would let me have a copy of the Deed under which the Board would accept the Guardianship.'

Studdert was in two minds: whilst wishing to divest himself of the responsibility for Bunratty he felt under some obligation to members of the local community; nor did he relish the prospect of his privacy being put at the mercy of large bodies of sightseers. 'If the key of the Castle should become absolutely at the disposal of the Board, and the Castle to be opened at any time to any person,' he told them on 19 May 1916, 'I am afraid this is an arrangement that I could not consent to as it would cause unpleasantness to me and other residents of the locality. If your surveyor would call, it might be possible to remove the dificulty.' The surveyor, in the person of Mr Salmond, duly called and discovered that Studdert was particularly worried about visitor access: 'He does not wish parties of 100 or 200 to be allowed in on a Sunday.' He also wanted to retain limited use of the ground floor, though agreeing that the stable could be vacated on a year's notice.

The board found itself in some difficulty in dealing with these

and Studdert's later conditions. He was understandably interested in profiting from the expected influx of visitors through
some percentage of admission fees. On this point, however, the
Commissioners pointed out that they could not charge admission to a monument of which they had been constituted
guardians, and indeed would have to consult legal opinion as to
whether they could levy such charges in the event of complete
vesting. Vesting, they further advised, would not automatically
give the public a right of access; but 'at the same time the Board
would not feel justified in spending public money on the Castle
unless the public were allowed reasonable liberty of access
thereto'. Studdert further compounded their difficulties in a letter of 24 October 1916 in which he asked the board's consent
that: 'a) The Castle to be kept strictly closed to the public on all
Sundays and general and local holidays, and also a few other

*Harold Leask's drawing of Bunratty as it appeared in 1941,
from his* Irish Castles and Castellated Houses

days which I would specify later; b) that I have a private key, and any member of my family have access at all times.' He also sought to retain the use of the basement turf store and permission to build on any addition to the castle 'provided no damage be done'. He further requested that 'the Castle be put to no commercial use, that no part be used for the benefit of any person; that any article brought to light be considered as my property, that the arrangement is cancelled on my refunding to the Board all the money spent on the Castle... I presume,' he concluded, 'that any change of Government would not affect the matter.' His letter further complicated the situation as far the commissioners were concerned by revealing that he was only tenant for life, and that the consent of the executors would have to be obtained for any alteration in Bunratty's legal status.

While this leisurely exchange of letters was taking place, events in Ireland had been moving rapidly. The Easter rising of 24 April and the subsequent execution of its leaders by the British authorities had ensured that there would be no return to the parliamentary debates on limited Home Rule; and in his concern about the possible effects of a change in government, Studdert was doing no more than reflecting the general uncertainty of the times. This was one point, nevertheless, upon which the board was not anxious to take a stand: 'It is difficult to say whether a change of Government would affect the matter,' they suggested cautiously on 28 October 1916. They were more immediately concerned, however, with the material matters raised in Studdert's most recent communication. They again sought legal opinion as to whether a tenant for life could be considered an owner under the terms of the 1882 Act, and the view taken was that Studdert would in fact have power to appoint the board as guardians. On 24 January 1917 they again wrote to him, concentrating on the key issue. 'The Board has no power,' they informed him, 'to surrender an Ancient Monument over which they have once been appointed guardians... the arrangement must, therefore, be a permanent one and unless you are prepared to carry it out as such, the matter cannot proceed further.' They also emphasised that they could not consent to any addition to the castle as contemplated; in fact it would be a condition that an area of ten feet of clear space be left all round the building to facilitate repairs and maintenance.

Studdert responded to this with a proposal that the board should give further consideration to his requests, but it was apparent that matters had reached an impasse. He made no further move until a year later, when in February 1918 he called on the commissioners in person in Dublin and assured them that he was willing to proceed with the vesting of Bunratty if the trustees of his estate and his brother should concur, and that he would be in touch with them on the matter. On the day of his visit, 27 February, County Clare was proclaimed a military area by the commander-in-chief of the British forces in Ireland; the whole county was heavily garrisoned, censorship of postal and telegraphic communications introduced and the local newspaper, the *Clare Champion*, first severely restricted and then entirely suppressed.

It was scarcely surprising that nearly another year was to pass before the board heard from Thomas Studdert again. 'I have not forgotten the matter,' he wrote, 'and am still rather inclined to vest the ruin, but, and I am afraid it is rather a large "but", the times are such that I do not care to make any decision at present... I am as anxious as you are to see the old ruin properly preserved, and it is quite possible that I may vest it sometime.' This letter was dated 23 January 1919. Two days previously the seventy-three Sinn Féin members returned in the landslide general election of the previous December had formed themselves into the first Dáil Éireann and issued a Declaration of Independence. By the time the matter of the preservation of Bunratty was again brought to the attention of the relevant authority, both it and the country it served were under new management.

By the year 1935, with the caustic experience of revolution and civil war now – though only barely – a thing of the past, the new state was cautiously assembling an individual identity. There were Turf Accountants, selling not fuel but dreams of gambling riches to those who had anything left to hazard after investing in the Irish Hospitals Sweepstakes, founded in 1930. The unarmed Gárda Síochána had replaced the hated RIC; Radio Éireann, set up in 1926, was boosting its revenue with commercially sponsored programmes; the colourful Blue Huzzars had made their first appearance in public at the Eucharistic Congress in Dublin in 1932. On a larger canvas the first steps towards a modern infrastructure had been taken with the completion of the huge hydro-electric scheme at Ardnacrusha, near Limerick, and the consequent establishing in 1927 of the Electricity Supply Board, the first of what was to become a substantial number of state-sponsored bodies. In other respects horizons were shrinking. In July 1929 the Censorship of Publications Act had become law and on 28 February 1935 the Criminal Law Amendment Act banned the importation of contraceptives. If it was to be, in the derisive term, a grocers' republic, there were those who were anxious to ensure that the goods on the shelves carried a distinctively Irish brand image.

This attitude was, however, by no means consistent. Ireland had pulled the first plank from under the British Empire, and as the pioneer post-colonial state, set the pattern for those that were to follow by paying the departing imperial power the compliment of retaining many of its institutions and apeing many more. The Office of Public Works fell within the former category. Created by an Act of Parliament in 1831, it was one of the oldest offices of state in Ireland and throughout the 19th century had been involved in a comprehensive range of largely uncontroversial and beneficial projects, from the building of schools, prisons and bridges to major civil undertakings such as the Shannon Navigation works. It was given a key role in Land Purchase under the first Land Act of 1870 and for many years was in effect the chief British government instrument for the implementation of economic policy in Ireland, particularly in the rural and agricultural areas.

The establishing of other bodies such as the Land Commission, the Congested Districts and Local Government Boards and the Department of Agriculture and Technical Instruction in the later 1800s and the earlier part of the 20th century had, however, relieved the Commissioners of Public Works – as the body was formally designated – of many of the more onerous of these duties, and allowed them to concentrate on the provision and maintenance of official buildings and the preservation of national monuments. This latter role had been created largely as a result of the disestablishment of the Church of Ireland in 1871, a move which was to result in the vesting in the board of some hundred disused churches and ecclesiastical buildings, formerly Church property, to be maintained as national monuments on account of their architectural merits or their antiquity. The vesting of the first of these, the monuments on the Rock of Cashel on 27 October 1870, marked the effective inauguration of the board's role in this sphere.

The existence of two acts of parliament (the 1869 National Monuments and the 1882 Ancient Monuments Acts) with separate financial arrangements, created, however, many difficulties for the Office of Public Works. Under the latter act, injury to a scheduled monument was punishable by fine or imprisonment, but was not enforceable against an owner unless he had appointed the commissioners as guardians. The Ancient Monuments Protection (Ireland) Act of 1892, though extending the range of buildings and monuments which the commissioners could accept from owners, still left them with inadequate powers to deal with those who proved to be hostile or unco-operative. When the new state came into being, legislation was introduced in the form of the National Monuments Act of 1930 which replaced all previous enactments and abolished the distinction between ancient and national monuments, broadening the definition of the new amalgamated category in respect of age (the classification had until then been restricted to prehistoric or mediaeval structures) and giving the board powers of compulsory purchase where an owner refused to sell. The act also set up a National Monuments Advisory Council to assist the Board of Works in its decisions and established the post of Inspector of National Monuments, hitherto held in conjunction with other responsibilities, on a full-time basis.

On 25 July 1935 Dermot Gleeson, of Clarecastle, County

Clare, wrote to the Director of the National Museum of Ireland, Dr A. Mahr. He was troubled by a conversation he had had with Sergeant Long of the Gárda Síochána stationed at Newmarket-on-Fergus. The subject of the conversation was Bunratty Castle. 'He tells me,' he wrote, 'that it is in imminent danger of very serious damage and that its interior has been allowed to get into a very shocking state so that it is offensive to *bona fide* visitors through the depredations of *mala fide* ones. He says that portions of the stonework containing some very curious figures have been and are being pulled down and destroyed and that if something is not done very serious damage will result to the whole structure. In addition, picnic parties are lighting fires in the Castle from any stray woodwork they can pull down and are leaving their litter and more offensive nuisance in the structure. The owner is one Mr Thomas Studdert who lives near by. He is a peculiar individual and would be difficult to deal with. He has a caretaker of sorts but locks are smashed and the whole position is very unfortunate.' Dr Mahr forwarded Gleeson's letter to the Inspector of National Monuments, H. G . Leask, 'knowing that it pushes in an open door with you'.

Harold Graham Leask, the son of an architect, had been born in Dublin on 7 November 1882. His early years with the Office of Public Works were largely spent in charge of its district office in Dundalk, County Louth, but on his promotion to the rank of Assistant Architect in 1920 he had returned to Dublin and taken over responsibility for the drawing office at 51 St Stephen's Green, the board's headquarters. In the years that followed he designed many significant city buildings, among them Pearse Street Gárda Station in rusticated granite, and was closely involved in the rebuilding of others, including the Four Courts, the Custom House and the General Post Office, following their destruction during the 1916-22 period. In 1923 he was appointed Inspector of National Monuments, a position he was to hold for twenty-six years. He had already developed a serious interest in mediaeval architecture whilst serving in Dundalk and, as far as he was concerned, the door to Bunratty and its future did indeed stand wide open. He reported to the board on 20 September 1935: 'Of the great interest of Bunratty Castle there can be no doubt.'

Thomas Studdert had in 1924 deferred any further consideration of the proposal of vesting, and there the matter had rested
until 24 August 1935 when the Clare County Council had passed
a resolution, forwarded to the Office of Public Works, that it
should take over and maintain Bunratty Castle as a national
monument and 'thereby prevent any further damage to the
premises'. Leask scarcely needed this prompting to revive the
issue. 'I have observed the building and occasionally visited it
when passing during recent years,' he wrote in his report, 'and
have noticed a progressive decay of the upper parts and that it is
high time that repairs were put in hand to preserve it from further decay. It is open, except for the basement vaults, to every
passer-by and is, I am creditably informed, often used as a dance
hall.' He expressed the view that it must be preserved and suggested that Studdert should again be approached on the proposal for guardianship. With regard to the likely cost of
preservation he estimated that 'as there is no serious structural
defect I think a sum of £600 would suffice'.

Studdert was written to on 9 October and the County Council
informed that the matter was receiving consideration. On 4
November the board requested observations from the National
Monuments Advisory Council, duly received on 9 December over
the signatures of the joint Honorary Secretaries, A. Mahr and H.
G. Leask. Not surprisingly, perhaps, the council informed the
board that they 'thoroughly approve of the proposal to take
Bunratty Castle into Guardianship and to an expenditure of £600
on its repair'. The way, however, was not yet clear. Under the act
the Commissioners were obliged to seek the authorisation of the
Department of Finance and made a formal application to this
effect as the year ended, supporting its request with a history of
the castle and a pencil drawing. It sought simply at this stage
authorisation to reopen negotiations with Thomas Studdert.

There the matter would appear to have rested for some eighteen months, but while Dublin deliberated Sergeant Long in
Newmarket-on-Fergus was keeping an anxious eye on developments – or the lack of them. A man with a keen interest in local

history and archaeology, he wrote in June 1937, signing himself S. Ó Longaigh, Árus An Gárda, to H. G. Leask, both on Bunratty and on the Holy Well at Kilmaleery. Of the former he said, 'Some ten years ago Mr Studdert gave the creamery manager permission to "fix up" one of the surrounding buildings of the ruins as a garage. He, however, refused to give him a lease or make anything permanent. The lower vaulted room is only being used for a matter of some weeks as a workshop for making butter boxes and as a store for butter... Re Mrs Ryan, the Ryans have been using one of the rooms under the Eastern Terrace for a lifetime but they have not been there as tenants or with anything more than the permission of Mr Studdert... .' The Ryans were proprietors of the licenced premises known to future generations as 'Dirty Nelly's' – in the early 1960s, at least, with some justification. The adjective was sanitised by the alteration of the vowel when it was subsequently sold and rebuilt.

Sergeant Ó Longaigh's professional duties clearly enabled him to keep a keen eye on the goings-on at the castle. 'I have just discovered,' his letter continued, 'that during the past three days a nephew of Mr Studdert, one Mr Russell, has been to Bunratty. He has directed his man to clean the place up a bit, to provide locks and chains for the door and the outer gate, and to leave the keys at the Public House of Mrs Ryan, at the Bunratty Bridge, for visitors. Mrs Ryan says she cannot take any responsibility for any damage done to the Castle. Today when passing I noticed Mr Russell's man cleaning up the place. I had put up a notice there threatening to prosecute any person found damaging the place. I would like to know from you if I may say you are really taking over the place or if it is remaining the property of Mr Studdert (or his successors). Much damage has been done to the walls etc. recently by persons who pull out supporting bricks in parts of the walls and dropping them on to the lower terrace as a form of recreation it would appear.'

Leask, in his reply, was only able to assure the sergeant that the case was being considered; but some three months later he again inspected Bunratty and furnished a comprehensive report. It offers a very clear picture of the contemporary condition of the later accretions to the castle proper, which is of considerable interest in the light of what was to follow. Leask reported:

1. The modern house on the W side, now roofless and internally ruined, could be excluded from the vesting and communications between it and the castle could be cut off, as when the house was in occupation, by the closing up of some openings in the west wall of the older structure. The house could be reconstructed without interfering to any great extent with the castle walls than was the case in former years. That is to say the older walls afforded support to floor and other beams and certain chimney flues of the house were and are incorporated in these walls. The house, moreover, could retain the small self-contained garden in front and the garden to the north but right of access to the castle walls or in parts of the area should be included in the vesting. In so far therefore as the house is concerned the Land Commission could be requested – if it appears that the Studdert successors persist in their proposals – to exclude the area surrounded by a green line on the plan hereunder. I am of the opinion that whatever rights or easements the owners had in respect of the house, i.e. rights of support, flues etc., would remain vested in them.

2. At E side another modern erection of 1 storey in height and vaulted fills the space between the towers on this side and projects considerably. Its roof is a flat concrete terrace approached by a steep flight of steps at the S end and forms the main way of approach to the Castle, the present entrance door being at the terrace level. It is a modern building of no antiquarian interest. Both this building and the lowest main storey of the castle, the vaulted basement, are used by the owner... . There is no objection, I think, to the continuance of the use of the basement... for the same purposes as heretofore. There is a precedent for a similar arrangement in the case of Dunsoghley Castle, Co. Dublin, where the tenant purchaser is permitted to use part of the Castle for storage purposes but not for housing animals... . It was to be noted that it was to provide for these circumstances that guardianship status was proposed by us.

In spite of this evidence that the family wished to retain the occupancy and use of certain areas of the castle, Leask recommended that the Land Commission be asked to vest it, agreeing the continued use of the lower vault with the owners. Before anything conclusive could be achieved, however, the storm clouds had again gathered and the event known in Ireland as The Emergency and elsewhere as the Second World War placed the undertaking of a major project such as the restoration of Bunratty Castle well down the list of priorities. Harold Leask's 1941 publication, *Irish Castles and Castellated Houses*, contains his own sensitive drawing of Bunratty from the south-east in the condition in which he had reported it some few years previously, but makes no mention of any projected restoration. Happily, before he died, aged eighty-one, in 1964, the long envisaged project had become a reality.

Even as Europe prepared for war, events were taking place in County Clare that were to shape the whole future of the Shannon region and its most important mediaeval castle. The first proving flights of what was to become a regular transatlantic flying boat service had operated from Foynes, on the Limerick shore of the Shannon estuary, in July 1937, at which time Rineanna, on the Clare side, was being developed as the future land-plane base. In 1942 a young County Clare man, Brendan O'Regan, was appointed by the then Minister for Industry and Commerce, Sean Lemass, to manage the restaurant at Foynes and subsequently that at the new Shannon airport. 'I think you can start the Bunratty scene at the very outset as far as I am concerned,' O'Regan said in 1990. 'It brought about a situation where seaplanes disgorged their passengers in Foynes and we put them on a bus and they were brought across to the land-plane base at Rineanna and then to the UK mainly.' That meant, he said, that they passed some interesting sites en route and Bunratty was the one which seemed to appeal to them the most. 'It was then a ruin, of course, and one that I would have known as a young fellow living in Sixmilebridge – we would have climbed this tree growing on the top and played handball against it and so on. Its impact on my mind was that it was something that was important to us in the future development of tourism, and the aviation age seemed to be our big chance to break through into American tourism particularly.'

A seed had been sown.

# As Big as the Fort Garry Hotel

'I REMEMBER HIS wife telling me that he rang her to say that he was coming home via Ireland,' Christopher Lynch recalled. 'I think the year would be around 1953. He arrived late one night on a British Overseas Airways flight at Shannon. It was his first time in Ireland and he got a taxi to Glyn's Hotel in Gort and arrived there late. And he always tells the story against himself that Michael, the night porter, met him and asked him to sign the register. So, as any peer would do, he just wrote G-o-r-t. And Michael looked at the register and said: "Look, if you don't go and sign your proper bloody name to that you'll go out on your ear." But anyway, he went off the following morning to look at Lough Cutra, seeing it for the first time. He had just heard about it in the family history, only to discover that Lough Cutra was sold for demolition.'

Colonel John Gillman, an old friend and later the Gort family's solicitor, remembered it differently. 'My wife and I were married in 1956. It was shortly before then and I was living with them. Lord Gort was not much away from home but he often used to go into Newcastle. On this particular day he returned and the first thing he did was to pick up the post and he would sit down in a rocking chair in a little room that he and his wife and I often used to frequent. On this particular day – this would be about five o'clock in the afternoon – he suddenly said, "Good gracious me, Lough Cutra's for sale – I think I'll go and buy it." The next morning he took an eight o'clock flight from Newcastle airport. On the evening of the same day he rang his wife to report progress and he said he'd bought Lough Cutra. That was it.'

Eastward from Winnepeg, Canada? Westward from Newcastle-upon-Tyne, England? The provenance may be disputed, but it was certainly true that Standish Robert Gage Prendergast Vereker, seventh Viscount Gort in the peerage of Ireland, was on that occasion, in his fifties, paying his first visit to a country with which he was closely connected by ancestry. Maurice, Lord of Prendergast in Pembroke, 'a right valiant captain' according to the chronicler Holinshed, had landed in Ireland with Strongbow in 1169. His descendant, Sir Thomas Prendergast, was created first Baronet of Gort on 15 July 1699. His daughter Elizabeth's second husband was Charles Smyth, for forty-five years MP for Limerick, and her son John Prendergast Smyth, born in 1741, was created Baron Kiltartan of Gort on 15 May 1810 and Viscount Gort on 16 January 1816. He died unmarried on 23 May 1817 and both honours devolved with remainder to his nephew, the Right Honourable Charles Vereker.

John Vereker, a native of Brabant in Holland, had been one of forty-nine army officers deprived of their commissions by Oliver Cromwell for expressing royalist sentiments. At the restoration of Charles II he was granted lands in compensation in County Cork. His descendants settled at Roxboro, County Limerick, in the early 1700s and began a long and sometimes acrimonious involvement in the administration of the city. The role of Freemen contains many of the Vereker name, from Connell, son of Sheriff Vereker, 10 October 1763, to The Honourable Charles Smyth Vereker, son of Lord Viscount Gort, 29 August 1823; in 1833 Alderman John served as the last of many Vereker mayors.

Charles Vereker, the second viscount, had been MP for Limerick in the Irish parliament, First Lord of the Irish Treasury and last constable of the Castle of Limerick. With his regiment, the Limerick Volunteers, he played a major role in the defeat of General Humbert's Franco-Irish forces during the insurrection of 1798. 'Not a very popular family in Limerick,' in the view of Christy Lynch, who started work at Shannon airport in 1947 as a timekeeper, 'because they held the balance of power in Limerick Corporation for a long number of years.' But after helping to defeat the cause of Irish independence, Colonel Charles Vereker voted against the union with Britain, offering the typically schizophrenic Anglo-Irish explanation to Lord Castlereagh that 'having defended my country with my blood, I shall not betray her with my vote'.

In the mid-1600s the Verekers had been granted lands at Gort, County Galway, confiscated from the O'Shaughnessys. When in 1817 the second viscount inherited the title and estates from his uncle he employed the Pain brothers of Cork to build Lough Cutra castle there to the design of John Nash. It bears a curious resemblance to East Cowes Castle in the Isle of Wight which Nash built for himself and which was to become a Vereker property on their leaving Ireland. 'They used it as their summer residence,' said Christy Lynch, 'and the Gort I knew used to talk about Queen Victoria having her house next door and as a child he used to see her with her chauffeur... she would be riding around in a pony and trap.' By 1842, when the third Lord Gort inherited Lough Cutra, the estate had become seriously encumbered, a situation exacerbated by the famine years, during which the Gorts were both unable and unwilling to collect their rents from a prostrate tenantry. In 1851 the Gorts left Ireland. The castle and demesne were sold to the Loreto Order for £17,000 and subsequently passed to Hugh Gough, a former ensign in Colonel Charles Vereker's Limerick regiment and by then a field-marshal. His grandson added a wing in 1895, but when in 1952 the seventh viscount stepped in to save it from demolition, Lough Cutra had lain unoccupied and neglected for twenty years.

Having bought it, Gort was at a loss to decide what to do with it. Neither he nor his wife had any intention of living there, and he had little interest in it in the architectural context. 'He wasn't a professional architect,' said John Gillman, 'but I would say that his knowledge of mediaeval architecture was quite as extensive as almost anybody, including professional people – he had made a study of it all his life.' Gort had inherited his house in County Durham, Hamsterley Hall, from his mother, whose father was Robert Smith Surtees, author of stories of the hunting field and creator of the character of Jorrocks. It was 'a very nice eigh-teenth-century house', in Gillman's estimation, 'not enormous as country houses go but large enough. It was, however, eighteenth-century Gothic. Now Lord Gort was not interested in anything Georgian, either architecturally or furniture or so on; and it wasn't long after he succeeded to Hamsterley [in 1933] that he began to introduce earlier features which... in a sense made it something not altogether accurate – an eighteenth-century house on which he superimposed stone windows, doors etc. which had come from houses two or three hundred years older than Hamsterley Hall.'

Gort had no such plans for Lough Cutra. 'Some of it was live-able and the stables there had been converted and they were live-able in,' recalled Joe McElgunn, who was then working in the Sales and Catering organisation at Shannon airport. 'But Gort, from his experience in Canada, saw the potential and the value of the woodlands... when he took over the estate at Hamsterley Hall it was in great debt, and he had to raise money. He devel-oped the woods and from the sale of the timber eventually paid off the money he borrowed and put the estate in credit again.' As for Lough Cutra: 'He wasn't the slightest bit interested in eighteenth-century architecture but he wanted to preserve the castle, maybe for his heirs... . He had no family, but there was the present Lord Gort who succeeded him and was in the back-ground somewhere.' In the event successive collateral members of the family lived in Lough Cutra until it was eventually sold and passed once again from Vereker ownership.

The Honourable Robert Vereker's passionate interest in mat-ters mediaeval was acquired early in life. 'Gort used to tell the story that his room in Cambridge was furnished by himself with mediaeval things,' recalled Christy Lynch. He made no academic study of the period, however: in fact he read law at Cambridge, a choice which continued to puzzle his friend John Gillman, who had first met him when both were in the British army: 'One day he said to me, "but I never bothered to go and collect the degree". The only principles of law which he remembered were some which had a touch of humour.' Gort's grandfather had been a solicitor, but Gillman could detect no other factor that might have induced him to follow the same course. He never practised – in fact, he was never gainfully employed in the common sense of the term. 'Lord Gort, of course, is extremely vague on all figures...' his London solicitor, G. H. Walford, wrote to Percy Le Clerc in December 1957; but he had early evinced a hard-headed business ability.

He had started buying property in Winnepeg as a young man as a result of a friendship that developed while he was at Trinity College, Cambridge, with Laurence Cadbury of the chocolate firm. They travelled to Canada together and Gort became very Canadian-minded, thereafter paying regular yearly visits, both on his own and later with his wife, which were interrupted only by the two World Wars. He was in Canada when the first war broke out and immediately joined the ranks of the Canadian army, returning subsequently to Britain and the commission that his social position made inevitable. He was mentioned in dispatches, but unlike his field-marshal brother, the sixth Viscount Gort – who was the only peer to win a Victoria Cross in the Great War and who became Chief of the Imperial General Staff in 1937 – was not temperamentally suited to the military life. He was very patriotic, said Gillman, but not really disciplined: 'Oh discipline is a fine thing – my brother loved it. It's all right for some people, but not for me.'

Gort developed an empathy for the rougher aspects of the Canadian way of life – he and his wife frequently went trekking in the Rocky Mountains – and eventually took Canadian citizenship. Although remaining intensely loyal to Britain, he 'never felt the same about the British since Churchill took the C-in-C command away from his brother', the *Limerick Sun* alleged on 15 January 1967. His Canadian business interests extended to coal mining and hotels and apartment blocks, in which he would stay on the occasion of his visits. 'Standish Robert Gage Prendergast Vereker, 8th [*sic*] Viscount Gort, comes to Winnepeg every summer,' reported the *Winnepeg Tribune* on 3 July 1958. '[He] stays at the Fort Garry Hotel, looks over his business property, then goes on west to his coal mines. He's a familiar figure in town, striding about hatless, his shirt sleeves rolled to his elbows, his jacket over his arm. After the war, when he succeeded his brother "Tiger" Gort, VC, hero of Dunkirk and North Africa, the tall, sturdy man bought an Irish castle "because it was a good buy. A castle in good condition is rare. Most of them have a side out or something. Only the woodwork was gone. You can go up the spiral staircase to the top of one tower, walk across the new roof behind the battlement, go down the spiral in the second tower. Bunratty Castle is as big as the Fort Garry Hotel, looks something like it... .'"

If there is some disagreement as to where Gort materialised from to acquire Lough Cutra, the sequence of events which led to his involvement in the restoration of Bunratty is now almost impossible to establish with absolute certainty. A number of individuals have claimed the credit – or had the credit claimed for them – for first interesting him in the crumbling monument. On the very first day of his first visit to Ireland, Christy Lynch believed, 'John Hunt caught up with him in Gort, and a day or two later he invited him to Limerick, where the Verekers originated, and, passing Bunratty, Gort admired the ruin... . So he showed him round and Gort was terribly impressed with Bunratty and went to the Studderts who owned the ruin. I think the deal was closed that evening. He bought Bunratty and an acre of ground for something like £1,000. And everyone thought, of course, that he was off his head.'

This impression was to persist. Some time later, Lord Gort took a bus from Limerick to Shannon. As they were passing the castle the bus conductor, not knowing who he was, said, 'Do you see that place there, sir? A fecking Englishman bought it for a thousand pounds to have it restored. Jesus, he really needs his head examined.'

If Bunratty was really an 'impulse buy' on Gort's part, the transaction was certainly not undertaken by someone in need of psychiatric care; nor was it signed and sealed then and there. According to Christy Lynch, when Gort rang Lady Gort at Hamsterley Hall that night and told her that he had bought not only Lough Cutra but Bunratty as well, 'she thought he had gone off his game'. On 5 June 1953 Gort wrote from Co Durham to Percy Le Clerc: 'We are buying it and I have paid 25% deposit and the whole thing will be completed in a few months. I saw Hunt and of course anything I do will be under the censorship of your department, but I have no wish to do anything out of order.' It is clear that he had proceeded with some circumspection, having been made aware, no doubt by John Hunt, of the close interest of the Office of Public Works in the matter; and having – a move of equal importance for what was to follow – obtained the approval and support of his wife.

Of the five individuals who were to play the key roles in the affairs of Bunratty – Lord and Lady Gort, Percy Le Clerc, Brendan O'Regan and John Hunt – it is the involvement of the latter that was to prove the most contentious. It is obvious that Gort would have known Hunt well before the question of acquiring of the castle ever arose. He was a leading antique dealer whose mediaeval interests paralleled Gort's and for some years they had been in professional contact, if no more. It was Hunt, according to Christy Lynch, who had sent Gort a cutting from a newspaper or magazine advertising the sale of Lough Cutra, which had brought him hot-foot from Canada: a version which, of course, does not accord with Gillman's recollections. 'They knew each other as Hunt and Gort,' recalled Christy Lynch; 'there were no christian names.' But this was the style of the time, and their association clearly went beyond that of a mutual commercial antiquarian interest.

If Hunt was undoubtedly one of the prime movers, there were those who suggested that he claimed credit beyond his contribution, and that Lord and Lady Gort were annoyed at the publicity he gained as a result of his involvement. That such varying recollections should have persisted is remarkable only in that they are not more numerous: the five principals who found themselves together planning the reinvention of Bunratty had each his or her own agenda; and though they were in clear agreement as to the practical outcome, the methods, the details and the emphases were another matter.

John Hunt was in many ways a Renaissance figure, a polymath

whose undoubted business acumen in the matter of buying and selling antiques was both grounded in and counterpointed by a formidable academic expertise in the field. A Limerick man, he had been brought up in London and returned in 1940 – he was of the same age as the century – to live in Lough Gur, County Limerick. He restored Craggaunowen Castle, County Clare, where he was to create a plausible replica of a *crannóg* – or lake dwelling – and ringfort. Further plans for a museum to house his collection of antiquities were inhibited by rising costs and were uncompleted at his death.

The Craggaunowen Project, commenced in 1973, 'was John Hunt's brainchild', wrote Patrick F. Doran in the commemorative issue of the *North Munster Antiquarian Journal* (1978) entitled 'Studia in Memoriam John Hunt', 'inspired by his desire to bring alive to the Irish people by a visual presentation their own cultural heritage, and in so doing to emphasise its place in the mainstream of European civilisation'. Hunt presented both Craggaunowen Castle and its grounds to the nation, together with his priceless collection of antiques, to be known as the Hunt Collection and housed in a specially-designed museum in Plassey House in the University of Limerick. Its ultimate location was planned for the old city customs house, to be specially restored for the purpose. He wrote widely on both furniture and artefacts and on archaeological matters, but his academic reputation rests largely on his two volume *Irish Mediaeval Figure Sculpture, 1200-1600*, published in 1974, two years before his death. The esteem in which he was held locally is reflected in the editorial to the 1978 commemorative publication: it was, it said, 'as a token of gratitude from the people of Thomond that this special number of our Journal is published in our benefactor's memory. John Hunt, together with his wife Gertrude, has given us something of unique importance, and it is with humility that we offer this in return.'

Hunt's entry in the second edition of *A Dictionary of Irish Biography* (1988), whilst reciting many of these facts, includes also the statement that 'He was responsible for the restoration of Bunratty Castle and the establishment of a "folk park" there';

whereas Craggaunowen, the article suggests, was restored only 'under his guidance'. It would appear that if Hunt had not himself claimed the prime role in Bunratty's restoration, he was not lacking in sympathisers willing to thrust it upon him.

With the restoration complete Desmond Guinness, founder of the Irish Georgian Society, arranged for him to give a lecture on the subject in Trinity College, Dublin. 'Hunt asked me could I lend him some slides,' Le Clerc recalled. 'I said would you like me to come and propose the vote of thanks – which I did. In his lecture he criticised some of the decisions I had made with Gort about removing all the extraneous things round the building, and I remember saying in my vote of thanks that no two people undertaking a job would do it in the same way.' After Hunt's death Le Clerc, encountering his widow at a reception, made the point to her that her late husband had never in fact himself claimed that it was he who had restored Bunratty. '"Ah, no," she said, "he was too modest!"'

Though in this matter Percy Le Clerc's professional standing was clearly at issue and his reaction is understandable, Lord Gort, in the memory of all who knew him, was the most generous and fair-minded of men, and if he were indeed annoyed at Hunt's apparent monopolising of the limelight, it can scarcely have been without reason. On the other hand, as Christy Lynch put it, 'only for John Hunt we would never have found Gort'.

*The Irish Times*, in an extended article on 30 May 1960 to mark the opening of the restored castle, attempted to be even-handed in the matter: 'There is no one else in these islands with his [Hunt's] particular feeling for the mediaeval and his capacity to read the significance of the objects and the uses to which they were put. One feels that just as Bunratty is a lasting tribute to the taste of the collector, Lord Gort, it is equally a justification of the knowledge of John Hunt.' The point that Hunt's critics would make in this context is that Gort's contribution extended to far more than a timely exhibition of good taste. As another of the protagonists, Brendan O'Regan, was to put it: 'We cannot repay him: he has added immeasurably to our heritage.'

This divergence of opinion is significant, not so much as evidence of stresses within a fortuitous alliance of strong individualists, as for the light it sheds on the assumptions with which the whole project for restoration was approached. Whatever else might be alleged of Hunt, there is ample evidence that his involvement was eminently practical. In May 1959, with the restoration nearly complete, Pa Crowe was asked by the contractor – an old school friend – to come down and work for a week. (He was still there in 1994.) 'So I came down,' Crowe remembered, 'and was introduced to a man, John Hunt.' Crowe was given the job of levelling and pointing the flagstones in the Great Hall. 'All these things were new to me but John Hunt was a fantastic man to work for. He had ways and means to make everything very easy.'

'He had a great presence,' in the view of Marcus Ó hEochaidh. 'And then he had this very extensive knowledge of European art and he had connections – and that was very important. For a while he was Mr Bunratty. He was on the National Monuments Advisory Council so therefore he was a very important ally as far as Percy was concerned.'

There is no suggestion, at the commencement at least, that Hunt had given Gort himself any cause for concern. 'John Hunt will have the best idea of my intentions subject to the restrictions of your department,' he wrote to Percy Le Clerc on 12 June 1953. And yet Peter Donnelly, who was working in Shannon Sales and Catering at the time and was later Secretary of SFADCo, the Shannon Development company, expressed his own reservations. 'The most important man I always felt was Percy, who had the vision of what could be made of the place. John Hunt's interest in Bunratty I always found to be a bit ambivalent... though I wouldn't like to say anything against him because he did an awful lot.'

'Gort was a lovely man,' Donnelly remembered. 'He had a funny way of shaking the head. He talked as if he hadn't any money at all. You didn't feel that he exuded riches and aristocracy and all the rest of it... you couldn't fault him in any way.' Whatever about the divergent views held on the role of John Hunt, there was near unanimity regarding the eccentric viscount and his hare-brained scheme amongst those with whom he most immediately came in contact.

'He was a lovely man to work with,' said Pa Crowe; 'for a man of his prestige he was very mild. Even if he wanted to go into a room he would ask me was it all right to go in.'

On the other hand 'he was gently eccentric but he had a very good brain,' Mrs Gillman suggested; 'he was no fool, but he was cute – he wouldn't rattle anybody if he could avoid it. He would find a way round it.' This propensity was to stand him in good stead in the long saga of Bunratty and in his relations with his collaborators, all of whom, whatever their differences, were willing to accord him their unqualified respect. As John Gillman put it, 'He was a most honourable man. I am sure he never did a dirty trick in his life. His wife was the same,' Gillman continued. 'She was a very efficient person.' This quality is amply evidenced in the scrapbook which Lady Gort kept of the progress of the Bunratty project.

She was Bessy Surtees – a distant cousin of Gort's – and when she married Robert Vereker in 1921 was very content to share a simple rural life with him: neither was interested in the social activities normal to their class and time. Gort, though a country-man, had no enthusiasm for hunting or shooting – he hated killing anything – and his main interests, which his wife reciprocated, were running his estate and acquiring early artefacts and furniture. 'He never threw anything away,' said Mrs Gillman. 'He had a mania for collecting anything.' Lady Gort, if not a hoarder on this grand scale, was an equal enthusiast; and if she did not possess her husband's deep knowledge of the mediaeval period and in fact inclined towards the mahogany of the 18th century, she was, in Christy Lynch's estimation, 'a woman of extreme good taste'. She immediately recognised the possibilities of Bunratty and was strongly of the view that her husband should undertake its restoration.

In the view of Joe McElgunn, Lady Gort was 'the power behind the throne. He would only take certain actions if he had her support. She was a very quiet, unassuming person, formidable in the beginning, because of her reticence, you know, but when we got to know her later on she was a delightful, wonderful person, and it was mainly through her influence that the castle was left to the nation.' This impression was supported by that of Tom Sheedy, who got a summer job as a schoolboy at Bunratty in 1961 – and stayed. 'She was the brains behind Lord Gort. He was a very soft man and would go with the flow. She would think ahead. She used to egg him on to find more things for us.'

In spite of Gort's comfortable financial circumstances, there were to be times when, for various reasons, funds ran out and the whole enterprise was in danger of foundering. Marcus Ó hEochaidh recalled one such occasion when the work was near-ing completion 'when Lady Gort came into Percy's office – Percy was away – and she had got her Williams & Woods dividend which was her Christmas shopping money [Williams & Woods was then a prominent Dublin commercial concern] and it was for the large sum of £2,000. She put her name on the back of it and passed it across the table to me for the Bunratty funding. That kept us going until February and Bord Fáilte money started flow-ing again then.'

For the Gorts the whole thing was, in one sense, a great game. 'So far as Lord and Lady Gort were concerned,' said John Gillman, 'there never was any question of it being a commercial enterprise or of their making any money out of it – they were not the least interested in that; and I think if one were asked the question what had they in mind, the only thing I can say is that they took it as a challenge.'

'When I got the job to set up the restaurant in Foynes,' said Brendan O'Regan in 1990, 'I sought advice with regard to the interior decoration. I had been brought to see a cottage in Lough Gur where John Hunt and his wife Putzel [Gertrude] were then involved in the Lough Gur excavations and I was really entranced by the interior decor... . The architect of the day was Desmond FitzGerald, brother of Garret's,[1] and so I had to convince Desmond FitzGerald and Tim O'Driscoll[2] and others that this was what we required. So from an early date I had a relationship with the Hunts and the recommendation in that report in 1950 that Bunratty should be restored could easily have come to me from John Hunt. I can't remember now, but I suspect it did.'

In 1950 O'Regan was one of sixteen Europeans who went to the USA to study what Americans would demand in terms of tourist facilities when they began, as was hoped, to cross the Atlantic in numbers. He had moved across the Shannon from Foynes to Rineanna (as Shannon airport was first named) in 1943 and continued to operate restaurants in both locations until flying-boat services were terminated three years later. At Rineanna, as head of the Sales and Catering organisation, he opened the world's first duty-free shop – a single counter reminiscent of a village store – and developed the restaurant to a standard unexcelled in the Ireland of the day, certainly outside the capital.

Foynes and Rineanna had been selected in 1935 as the location for combined sea- and land-plane terminals, and it was not until the post-war period, with large numbers of surplus aircraft coming on to the market, that a new flying-boat base to be built as part of the Rineanna development and to supercede Foynes was finally abandoned. The initial harbour construction works are still in evidence. Rineanna, with the land-plane having established its dominance, functioned as a mandatory fuelling stop for all transatlantic flights: in the late 1940s and early '50s it was serving seven international airlines and its restaurant was open twenty-four hours a day, not only serving meals on the ground but providing in-flight catering. Already, however, there were growing apprehensions: US airlines in particular were pressing for direct access to Dublin (denied them under a 1945 Bilateral Agreement) in what were to prove the first moves in a long-running campaign. It was generally acknowledged that the new generation of jet aircraft with their greatly increased range would be able to overfly Shannon and render a substantial investment, both in economic and social terms, virtually redundant.

O'Regan and his small Sales and Catering team were charged by the then Minister for Industry and Commerce, Sean Lemass, to seek every means to mitigate the effects of this eventuality.

The response of the Shannon Development Authority, a scratch organisation without statutory status, derived from the existing Sales and Catering organisation and drawing its members from it, was to develop on two fronts. In 1947 Shannon had become the world's first customs-free airport, and though its envisaged role as an entrepôt for the transhipment of goods had remained largely unfulfilled, the energies of O'Regan's small team were now directed to attracting major multinational companies to set up on its industrial estate. This initiative met with considerable success and led in turn to the creation of a new town in the airport hinterland to house their employees. The other perceived area where development appeared to be possible was tourism, with a strong emphasis on the largely untapped United States market. O'Regan was accompanied on his 1950 visit to that country by representatives of Bord Fáilte, to which body he had been appointed by the inter-party government of 1948-51. Together they visited Williamsburg and Stourbridge which, said O'Regan, 'was quite an eye-opener in regard to the intense interest of the Americans in the past'. On his return O'Regan prepared an independent report which contained a recommendation that Bunratty Castle should be restored.

This bare summary conveys nothing of the climate in which these far-reaching plans were being assembled. The Ireland of the 1940s was epitomised in the American Paul Blanshard's book *The Vanishing Irish*, which predicted that, with emigration running at levels unprecedented since the Great Hunger of the 1840s, the country would soon be emptied of all but the very young and the very old. The principal cause was the lingering effects of the Second World War, during which Ireland, though neutral, had drifted into an economic backwater and found itself unable to maintain and renew its essential infrastructure. This resulted in serious post-war under-employment and lack of opportunity; though, in the view of the poet Patrick Kavanagh and his brother Peter, who together wrote and produced a short-lived publication, *Kavanagh's Weekly*, in the early 1950s, the causes were not exclusively economic. 'Why are the people leaving the countryside in their thousands?' they asked. 'They go to

England where the conditions are extremely bad. What they are seeking is the enthusiasm for life.'

Certainly there seemed to be little cause for enthusiasm, and thus little manifestation of it on the part of those dwindling numbers left behind. There was a strong sense, in T. S. Eliot's phrase, of 'living and partly living', the pervasive presence of what would later be characterised as a Beckettian hopelessness made all the more profound by the hyper-puritanical and joyless attitudes of the Catholic Church and many organs of state, the most calamitous of which was possibly the Censorship Board. The inter-party coalition, an unstable alliance of right and left which had assumed power in 1948 after sixteen years of Fianna Fáil rule, seemed bent, in the cause of fiscal rectitude (or in some cases of pure political spite), on demolishing those few signposts to progress which had been erected, or at least turning them to point in a different direction. The planned Aer Lingus service to North America was abandoned with the newly acquired aircraft literally ready for take-off. De Valera, out of office, set off, after years of diplomatic silence, on a futile worldwide crusade against Partition, while at the same time the long-range radio transmitter planned to link Ireland with its ever-growing diaspora was summarily abandoned.

Happily there were a few lights still flickering in the circumambient darkness, many of them located in the state sector. Sean Lemass, in setting up these bodies to take on roles that private industry was either unwilling or unable to assume, had picked his men well. J. F. Dempsey in Aer Lingus, C. S. Andrews in Bórd na Móna, the peat authority, M. J. Costello in Siúcre Éireann, the sugar company, combined a hard-headed business approach with a strong sense of national dedication, qualities possessed in equal measure by the young Brendan O'Regan. Trained in hotel management in Switzerland and at the family-owned Old Ground Hotel in Ennis, he was organising the catering services in Dublin's St Stephen's Green Club when Lemass came across him. Shrewdly assessing his potential, he offered O'Regan the job in Foynes and the two men established a close working relationship. When the Shannon crisis loomed O'Regan was told that he could spend £50,000 of the profits of Sales and Catering on developing new ideas: 'I got *carte blanche* from Lemass to do whatever could be done to stop the overfly.'

He put together a small team which included Joe McElgunn as tourist manager, J. C. Lynch as accountant and Peter Donnelly with responsibility for publicity and development promotion. With the return of Fianna Fáil to government in 1951 Lemass had appointed O'Regan chairman of Bord Fáilte, a move which considerably strengthened his hand; but the real impetus was very much local, developing over time into a strong sense of regional identity that often found itself at odds with what appeared from the Shannon perspective as over-centralised government. The atmosphere in Shannon from the beginning, O'Regan believed, was one of great creativity, or, more explicitly, of creative tension – a quality that was to characterise the circumstances in which the reinvention of Bunratty was undertaken and succcessfully carried through.

'As far back as I can remember,' said O'Regan in 1990, 'the compulsion for the restoration of the castle came from two angles. One was that Lord Gort had already collected a pretty fine lot of furniture that would be suitable for the restoration of a fifteenth-century castle, and the other was that we had a compulsion in Shannon to find a dramatic way of using it. These two things came together.' The Board of Works, which was to handle the actual restoration, had already been involved in the construction of the airport facilities, 'so there was a coming together of willingness at that level'. The board's interest in Bunratty had, as has been seen, long antedated the future variously envisaged for it by O'Regan, Hunt and the Gorts. It had proved impossible to come to an agreement, however, with Thomas Studdert, and the advent of the war had in any case brought about a situation in which no further progress could be made. In the mean time the interest in the property had passed to Studdert's nephew R. H. Russell, a retired tea-planter, who had expressed himself as willing to resume negotiations on the transfer of Bunratty to state care. These negotiations had already reached an advanced stage by the time Gort expressed an interest in acquiring the castle. In a letter to Russell dated 16 November 1951, Percy Le Clerc had written: 'I am very pleased to find that the difficult situation at Bunratty is now at last being solved and look forward to getting a start made on the works there.' The 'works' envisaged were at this point basically those of conservation, as recommended in Leask's earlier report. The sale of Bunratty to Gort was to alter the whole scope and complexion of the undertaking.

In 1962, two years after the re-opening, Le Clerc addressed the Thomond Archaeological Society on the subject of Bunratty. 'Full-scale restoration is an undertaking that needs very special circumstances to justify it,' he told his audience. 'It is most important not to submerge the genuine old work in a great quantity of new work... . The work also demands humility on the part of the restorer – a profound respect for the work of the original architect.' Le Clerc, who had succeeded Harold Leask as Inspector of National Monuments in 1949 after serving for a year as his assistant, was, in Joe McElgunn's estimation, 'a very nice guy if you knew him, but rather inclined to be withdrawn a bit: you could never get very close to him'. He was 'a very gentlemanly fellow who felt he had to ensure that the interests of the OPW were adhered to to the letter... any interference with the fabric of the building was frowned upon'.

This attitude was perfectly in accordance with the OPW remit. When Lord Gort bought Bunratty, Le Clerc said in 1990, 'we had just taken the ruin into guardianship.[3] Now in those days the Board's idea of looking after a ruin was to secure it as in the condition it was found, not to restore it, and so therefore as it was in State guardianship Gort naturally got in touch with us to know whether we would think of restoring it. Well, I took on the idea with great enthusiasm.'

That the enthusiasm on the part of the board's inspector was not always unconditionally endorsed by his employers was to become apparent. 'I don't think they cared a damn,' Le Clerc said in 1994. 'That was the trouble between me and the Board of Works: I was too earnest and they were too uninterested. I don't think we ever understood each other.' At that time, he said, the board were making out that the National Monuments Act as it stood then precluded them from undertaking restoration. 'Well, if it precluded the Board of Works from undertaking restoration it also precluded the Inspector of National Monuments from undertaking restoration! In other words, what I did at Bunratty was in addition to my official duties and unpaid.'

Le Clerc's insistence that the integrity of the 15th century elements of the castle should be preserved at all costs was in some eyes too radical a solution in view of his handling of its post-16th-century accretions. 'The English school of thought was to preserve the history of the building,' he said; 'if one did that at Bunratty the architectural confusion wasn't going to teach the Irish people and encourage them to take an interest in 15th century architecture – it was a mess.' In this context he regarded Bunratty as 'the Chartres, you might say', and justified his approach on these grounds.

What might be termed his proprietorial attitude gave rise to further tensions among those most closely involved with the project. At a later stage, when it was suggested that the basement hall should be refloored with Liscannor flag, McElgunn recollected, 'a bit of digging was done on it and they found something of archaeological interest. John Hunt had applied for a permit – a licence to excavate the basement – but didn't get it immediately. There was some delay and I recall it gave rise to a rather delicate breakdown in relationships (corrected later by Brendan O'Regan) because John Hunt went ahead and excavated the basement. Now nobody knows what, if anything, was found... . I think there might have been a personality clash between himself and Percy Le Clerc and some people in the Office of Public Works... . This strained relationships for a while but was finally corrected by O'Regan writing to the Office of Public Works and saying that while he knew that Hunt had applied for a permit, he had no knowledge that any digging had taken place or had continued, and he apologised profusely and stated that he had strongly advised Hunt in future that anything in regard to the fabric or the building would have to be processed through his office.'

There is no record of this incident on the relevant OPW file, but Pa Crowe and others confirmed that such an excavation by Hunt did in fact take place. If it had its significance in terms of the personalities involved, Le Clerc's working premise that Bunratty should re-emerge as a pure 15th-century building, shorn of all later additions, invited more fundamental disagreement. 'In Ireland there were no mediaeval buildings (other than ecclesiastical) in anything like their original condition,' he told the Thomond Archaeological Society, 'and I had for some years considered it desirable to take a small number of buildings of different types at different periods and restore them so that the visitor would then see more clearly what the ruins would have been like.' As regards Bunratty's 17th and 18th century additions, 'luckily none of these were of any great archaeological interest, but this shows how restoration always involved a certain amount of destruction; the whole operation can only be justified as a balance of gain over loss. When the late work had been removed, the fifteenth and sixteenth century fabric stood unencumbered and the work of interpreting, and deducing from often quite small clues what missing parts of the original work were like, could begin.' Not only did this radical approach call in question the OPW's hitherto standard policy of conservation of a ruin in the state in which it was found, but some critics suggested that the balance of gain over loss was not as apparent as Le Clerc seemed to assume.

For his part, the inspector was ready to admit that he regarded Bunratty as a subject demanding special treatment: 'My feeling was that in this particular case one should try and get back to the one period. Now this isn't always the right thing to do with a restoration, but in this case I felt it was justified' – justified, he explained, because there was no surviving castle of the period to equal it and because 'the fifteenth century was a very, very fine period of Irish architecture... . It has qualities very much of its own and therefore is important in the history of Irish civilisation. Now all the castles and indeed abbeys that were built in the fifteenth century were either in ruins or they had been so changed that you wouldn't know what they would look like originally, and

Bunratty was no exception to that.' He had previously considered taking a small tower house and restoring it fully – that is, returning it as far as possible to its architectural identity as originally built – but 'when Lord Gort appeared on the scene and suggested restoring Bunratty what were we to do? Tell him to go away with his money?'

Before this opportunity presented itself, however, Le Clerc's radical approach had already been clearly set out in an internal report to his board following an inspection on 16 February 1952. Though this, of course, did not envisage anything like the comprehensive restoration and refurnishing that was to eventuate through the involvement of the Gorts, Hunt and O'Regan, it made clear Le Clerc's desire to get back to basics. His report recommended, *inter alia*, the following:

A. Demolitions. Remove 18th-19th century brick and stone buildings from the four sides.

B. Corner Towers. Concrete over brick vaults at top, secure parapets, wall tops and gutter stones, repair steps of stairs and provide concrete roofs. Remove ivy, vegetation and vegetable soil. Rake out and point wall surfaces. Secure loose masonry, remove later brick buildings and flues and make good masonry. Open blocked windows and repair damaged opes. Provide concrete access galleries at wall walk level. Concrete over floors, reinstate access stairs. Restore approximately 6 yards super. of 17th century plaster in chapel...

C. Upper and Lower Hall

Vault. Clean out etc. and locate and reinstate original entrance.

Upper Hall. Provide protective roofs over remains of 17th century plasterwork etc.

Lower Hall. Repair and secure fireplace. Clear and repair 3 windows. Repoint etc.

Rooms at S and N ends. Similar.

Outside. 3ft wide strip of gravel around castle. Provision of 2 stiles and notices.

The total cost was estimated at £4,000. On 14 November 1952

a scaled-down estimate proposed roofing only ten feet of the Main Hall to preserve the plasterwork from the weather and covering the turrets with roofing felt and concrete slabs.

Before the board could act on these figures, however, events had taken another direction. In May 1953 a letter from J. Sexton, a Limerick solicitor, to Le Clerc informed him that Desmond O'Malley, another Limerick solicitor, was acting for Lord Gort in the matter of the purchase of the castle. This was followed on 5 June by an enthusiastic letter from the purchaser himself: 'I think it is a most wonderful castle. I will try and get say at least another 3 or 4 acres of land out of Russell. It would be nice to get the site of the earlier castle as well if we can.' The indenture made between 'Richard Henry Russell of the 1st part, the Agricultural Credit Corporation Limited of the second part and Lough Cutra Estates Limited of the third part' is dated the 30th day of October 1953. Under its terms Lough Cutra Estates, representing Lord Gort's interests, became 'absolutely seized of an estate of inheritance in fee simple... created by an Indenture of Fee Farm Grant dated the 26th day of September 1712 and made between The Right Honourable Henry Earl of Thomond of the one part and Thomas Amory of the other part...'. By a Deed of Guardianship dated 3 November 1954 the Commissioners of Public Works were appointed Guardians of Bunratty Castle under the National Monuments Act 1930. The parties to the deed were the Commissioner of Public Works, Richard Henry Russell and Lough Cutra Estates. Finally the stage was set.

## Notes

[1] Garret FitzGerald, after a career in Aer Lingus, the national airline, entered politics and became Taoiseach in 1981.

[2] T. J. O'Driscoll, then of the Aviation Section of the Department of Industry and Commerce, was closely involved with the early development of Irish civil aviation and of Shannon. He was subsequently director-general of Bord Fáilte, the tourist board.

[3] His recollection was at fault here.

# A Jigsaw of Scattered Stones

'WOULD YOU TELL your mistress that it's Mr Le Clerc and Lord Gort?'

The first time that the two met they retired after a preliminary inspection of the castle – 'to see what could be done', as Le Clerc put it – to Corbett's Hotel opposite. As they clambered round the ruin, 'I was saying what I would propose. And he would say, "Now, what will we do here?" And I'd say, "Well, I'm not quite sure about that"; and he would say, "Oh well, that will transpire!"'

Corbett's was then known as the Castle Hotel. 'My grandfather came here in 1878,' said Paddy Corbett. 'Before us there was a family called the Dawsons and they owned about four hundred statute acres. All these lands round here were owned by the Anglo-Irish.' In 1948 Paddy's parents began extending their residence, Bunratty House, and opened it the following year as an hotel. The oldest section of the house, dating from about 1790, had served as a boys' school, with the main part being added about the time that the Studdert's house (which has since taken over the 'Bunratty House' name) was built. The hotel attracted a regular clientèle from Limerick and Ennis. 'They were our faithful customers all down through the years,' said Paddy Corbett; 'they used to come out Saturdays and Sundays and every evening after their supper for their drink. It was like one big family – everyone knew everyone else.' For their overnight trade the Corbetts relied on custom generated by Shannon airport, and before the Shannon Shamrock opened in 1959 they played host to many in transit celebrities: Paddy recalled at random the screen actress Jennifer Jones and her husband David O. Selznick. Lord and Lady Gort became regular visitors. 'A thorough gentleman,' according to Paddy's brother, Dom Corbett. 'I knew Lady Gort very well too: her drink was a gin and orange.'

Percy Le Clerc had stayed in Corbett's himself on several occasions and knew it as a place where one could get an excellent lunch. When, after their first joint inspection, the two men went into the bar for an aperitif he asked the girl if he could order lunch for two, to be told that they only served residents. Lord Gort's interjection, however, put a different complexion on the situation, and lunch was forthcoming. 'People had heard he had bought the ruin,' said Le Clerc, 'though nobody had seen him at that stage.' The change of heart on the part of the hotel management was fortunate, since at the time there was nowhere else to eat between Bunratty and Limerick. And as for Bunratty village itself, 'There was a post office,' Le Clerc recalled, 'and there was one cottage, and there was Corbett's and there was Miss Ryan who owned the little pub... there were so few people and, you know, it all made quite a stir. So the poor girl when he said "Lord Gort" nearly fell apart and said, "Yes, I'll go and see." So then he turned to me and he said, "That should do the trick."' It did.

The inspection of the castle had revealed a fairly sorry state of affairs. 'It was really pretty far gone,' said Christy Lynch. 'I used to play handball there as a teenager and there were several of the steps missing from the stairs. The main guard – that floor was intact but it was covered with about a foot of cow dung and goats' droppings.'

Brendan O'Regan's recollections were similar: 'There was a timber stairs almost where the gallery is now where the meal is held. There had been a great tragedy there in fact before we came – a fellow had hung himself. But it was a wreck – the whole place was a wreck. There was no roof of course, and there were trees growing and piles of rubble and so on... but the stairs were good and you could get on to the towers, up on to the battlements.'

It was Paddy Corbett who, in October 1953, had discovered the suicide. 'We used to play handball there every Sunday and I went down on Saturday to clean the ball alley – it was half-way up the castle – and I had my dog with me, a pointer. He went up the circular staircase to the very top: I didn't miss him at all. The next thing I heard him crying and I called him but he wouldn't come down. So when I was walking up the stairs I saw the two legs hanging down...'

To the local eye, however, Bunratty was not quite the wreck of O'Regan's recollection. 'There wasn't that much wrong with the castle,' said Paddy Corbett. 'There was a lot of work in it – filling in bits and pieces where stones had been pulled out – but I think if it was done nowadays it would have been a relatively small job.'

Le Clerc's practical conclusions suggested a condition somewhere between such diametrically opposed views. 'There was no roof and all the battlements had gone. The main wall-walks more or less did remain. The space between the two towers on the north side – that's what we call the North Solar – that had been completely filled in so that the north front was flat, there was no recess where the present entrance is. And there had been a double stair outside – we could see the remains of it, the marks of it on the wall... a sort of formal symmetrical external stair leading up to the first floor entrance. And then inside they had gutted the north wall where the present entrance is and had put in a stair which by this time had disappeared and all there was was a sort of temporary stair that led up out of the paved hall.'

Percy Le Clerc had 'hit on the figure of six thousand' as the sum appropriate to remedying this sorry state of affairs; but this represented, in accordance with the perceived remit of the Board of Works, only the putative cost of conservation, not restoration. The board's officials, moreover, were understandably cautious in committing public monies to a project of this magnitude without assuring themselves of the *bona fides* of the new owner, lord or no lord. Marcus Ó hEochaidh recalled a certain commissioner of the time saying, 'Well, we're not going to spend even sixpence on a paintbrush until that man Lord Gort has signed and sealed that he is going to transfer it to the State afterwards. I hear he's a bit of an entrepreneur in Winnepeg.' (Though, Ó hEochaidh admitted, 'entrepreneur' would not at that time have been the word he employed.)

'We had to agree to show it – that was the terms,' Gort told the *Winnepeg Tribune* in 1958. 'We expect tourists from Shannon Airport – it's close by.'

Difficulties over funding were to be recurrent thoughout the period of restoration. Gort was a millionaire, said Le Clerc, 'and could have dipped into his pocket as deep as he wished. But you don't become a millionaire by throwing your money around, so he managed to hold back and persuade Bord Fáilte to take a financial interest in the work... but each of them tended to hold back saying they wouldn't put up any more money, hoping the other would then come up with it; and the result was we had to close the works twice and take down the scaffolding.' But in 1954 these problems lay in the future.

More immediate concerns, from Le Clerc's point of view, were those of persuading his employer that a radical departure from established practice was in this case both desirable and necessary. 'By degrees the Office of Public Works got drawn into it through Le Clerc's interpretation of his responsibility to the structure of the building,' said his former assistant Ó hEochaidh. 'We can't conserve it if we don't know what's there. Therefore we have to dig. But if you dig you disturb. And therefore if you disturb you should examine the disturbances. This was the philosophy that was applied.'

It was largely a matter of playing it by ear. The OPW, in Ó hEochaidh's view – and it should be remembered in this context that both he and Le Clerc were to resign from the board's service in the 1970s in an atmosphere of some acrimony – remained unwilling partners in the enterprise: 'And that's a tribute to Percy. He did a lot of this outside the requirements of the post activity.'

All of it, according to the man himself: 'What I did at Bunratty was in addition to my official duties and unpaid.' There was also, he added, the problem that 'nobody had done anything like this and there was nobody in Ireland with whom I could discuss problems and possible solutions. I used to come to France [where he had been living for ten years when he made this comment in 1994] and went to the monuments people in Paris, and used to travel with them: but again at my own expense and during my holidays.'

So the young architect knocked at the door of the Historic

*'Pretty far gone': the castle interior in December 1954*

Monuments Service in the Rue de Valois in Paris and explained who he was. 'I had a meeting with the great chief inspector Jacques du Pont. And I remember they asked me what was our annual budget for national monuments in Ireland. At that time it was 1000 francs approximately to the pound. And I said it was five million francs. They said no, you must mean five million pounds and I said no – and they all just burst out laughing. It was about the price of a three-bedroom semi.' The French connection was to prove doubly valuable: 'I hadn't any contact with anybody else who was actually doing a restoration and some practical points must have got through. And philosophical points – what is permitted.' He had also participated in two International Castles Institute study tours in Italy, meeting the distinguished architect Professor Gazzola, 'and having long discussions with him and other experts about the technical and ethical problems of architectural restoration.' Of the ICI itself he wrote, 'The fact that there was an international body concerned to establish and maintain sound principles and high standards of technique helped to make up for the absence of any such recognised standards in Ireland and made it possible to resist most of the undesirable pressures that were exerted by outside interests during the course of the works.'[1]

Le Clerc was an admirer of the French architect and restorer Viollet-le-Duc, who had renovated Pierrefont for Napoleon III – 'He died before it was finished but if he had gone into residence he would have hated it.' Viollet-le-Duc's approach involved almost complete rebuilding in the manner of the 'restorations' perpetrated on the cathedrals of Christ Church and St Patrick in Dublin in the 19th century, and Le Clerc was certainly not disposed towards such a radical solution. On the other hand, as he suggested in the Italian article already cited, 'At Bunratty, conservation would have only given a permanent record of the defacements of the building, which would not have served any useful purpose; what was needed in Ireland was a castle restored in large measure to its original condition, which would throw light on all the other castles of the period that were in ruins.'

If Le Clerc had a very clear idea of the result he hoped to

achieve, Gort began cautiously, feeling his way in this new situation. His letter of 5 June 1953, like all the others to the Inspector of National Monuments that have survived, was written in his vigorously rotund hand on Hamsterley Hall paper. 'I presume if the castle is shown people can still live in it with suitable furniture,' he hazarded, 'and that we can put in some plumbing under great restraint. I have some Gothic pictures on gold grounds as old as the castle, several Gothic clocks and some rather good large 15th century tapestries and I feel that all these would be very effective if it is to be a show place.'

Le Clerc, in his reply four days later, was equally circumspect: 'There are a number of points that will have to be approached from the right direction if the whole matter is to go smoothly.' He believed that it would be possible to make a clerk of works available that autumn and that the work would take twelve months.

In the event the caution proved to be amply justified and the estimate wildly optimistic; but while the first of the bureaucratic obstacles were being negotiated, Gort continued to formulate his plans. 'My idea was to make perhaps the north end habitable in course of time and to get someone living there so as to have it occupied if anybody will stand the 15th century atmosphere,' he wrote to Le Clerc on 12 June. 'There must, however, be a modern lavatory and bathroom somewhere... . The rest I would hope to furnish very sparsely perhaps but suitably. I have quite a lot of early things, 15th century and early 16th century... . I feel that the result should be very good if not taken too far.'

It was, of course, the question as to how far the whole thing should be taken that was causing concern in St Stephen's Green. The idea of treating a national monument as a tourist attraction was, as far as the Board of Works was concerned, totally new. Le Clerc recalled his predecessor, H. G. Leask, as having 'a very academic approach.... I was his assistant for about a year and I remember saying something about access for tourists. His reaction was, "We're not interested in tourists." It was a very pure approach: we were just interested in preserving antiquities – we didn't care whether anybody came to look at them. And the public reacted very much in the same way, reciprocally. They didn't take any interest in them.'

It is difficult, at this distance, to blame the OPW for doing little to break this particular vicious circle. A debate was already in train in June 1953 regarding possible admission charges and their admissibility under the terms of the act, but six years later, with work on the restoration yet to be completed, T. E. O'Donnell, a Limerick solicitor involved in a proposed Bunratty management agreement with SFADCo, wrote, *inter alia*, to Joe McElgunn: 'I think that the charge for admission of 2/6d. [12.5p. – about the then price of a pint of stout] is entirely too high and may be a deterrent to prospective visitors to the Castle. I imagine myself that 75% of visitors will in fact be Irish people and I put myself in the category of one who would like to assist in promoting interest in the Castle. I would have no hesitation in taking my family there for a trip on a Saturday or Sunday afternoon and paying say 1/- [5p.] per head entrance fee but 2/6d. per head would be out of the question... we must face the fact that one or two visits to the Castle by the ordinary individual would suffice for all time. A trip there to the average person would be similar to reading a book or seeing a picture. In other words once you have read it or seen it once, there is little desire if any to read or see it again.'

Lord Gort, for his part, had accepted the requirement that visitors, if any, should be admitted, though 'my idea was to make a charge if I am allowed to for upkeep really'. He was more concerned, understandably, with the practicalities and in his letter of 12 June 1953 hinted shrewdly at a *quid pro quo*: 'I will not promise to roof the great hall but certainly hope to. I think if we cut some Loch Cutra oak it will save us a lot of money... . If we fail to roof the great hall the place is still a partial ruin.' He then suggested that the OPW might take on the restoration of Lough Cutra castle 'while it is easily done... . I personally am not interested in Regency but I am doing my best to preserve the Castle as it is.'

There were still, however, legal matters to be resolved with regard to the acquisition of the property. The indenture conveying ownership to Lord Gort was signed on 30 October 1953. On 20 March 1954, John Hunt was writing to Percy Le Clerc from

Lough Gur: 'Gort is coming over on Thursday night and we are meeting him at the Inchiquin wedding on Friday... . He tells me he has bought some doors which will be very good indeed at Bunratty. The problem of the tenancy has been successfully solved and I understand the place is now vacant, so I think it would be as well for you to start before someone else moves in. I hear already that they are starting to use it as a handball alley and if we do not begin work soon they will establish a traditional right!' With the signing of the Deed of Guardianship in November, it seemed that at last the plans of the Gorts, Hunt and Le Clerc could begin to be translated into reality.

There was to be another hiatus, however, of almost three years, in the space of which further legal moves took place. By Indenture of Conveyance dated 11 October 1955 'all the fee simple estate and interest of Lough Cutra Estates Limited in the hereditaments and premises granted by the said Indenture of 30th day of October 1953 became vested in Lord Gort' and the following year, on 16 July 1956, John Hunt and Desmond J. O'Malley were appointed trustees of Bunratty, the Indenture of Settlement requiring them to hold the property on trust 'for Lady Gort for her life and after her death for the Right Honourable Jacqueline Corinne Yvonne Viscountess de L'Isle' – wife of the first Viscount de l'Isle and only daughter of Gort's late brother the field-marshal. 'Lord Gort vested the castle in his wife... with the intention that it would pass on to his heirs after that,' Christy Lynch recalled; but these were only the opening moves in what was to emerge as a complex legal chess game in which Brendan O'Regan's *ad hoc* Shannon task force was to play a key role.

In the mean time, however, Percy Le Clerc finally found himself in a position to begin work on Bunratty, and on 1 March 1957 Thomas Kavanagh moved on to the site as the OPW's clerk of works with responsibility for the restoration project. 'Thomas Kavanagh, who did the day-to-day supervision, was a very good, well-trained carpenter,' said Le Clerc, 'so then it was a matter of finding labourers, finding carpenters, and telling them how to do it.'

Above: *Work in progress, June 1957: the North Solar from the west wall walk.*
Below: *The new roof of the Great Hall under construction, June 1957*

*The new roof from the Great Hall interior*

One of the factors complicating the involvement of Shannon Development (as SFADCo came to be known) in the plans for Bunratty was that it did not then exist, properly speaking. As recorded in its report on activities for the period November 1957 to 31 July 1958, 'In the preliminary stages the Authority was an Organisation superimposed on the existing Sales and Catering Service... as at present the Authority has no legal existence.' This situation was not remedied until 28 January 1959, by which time the work of restoration was well under way.

Until an agreement between the interested parties could be formalised, however, there was no guarantee of funds being made available to complete the work. On 4 November 1959 John Hunt had written to Brendan O'Regan: 'I am so anxious as you know to get the position with regard to an agreement between the Shannon Authority and Bunratty settled because until I do, Bord Fáilte will not make the funds voted allready [sic] available, and Percy Le Clerc I am afraid will get tired of waiting.'

These legal anomalies had not, nevertheless, inhibited O'Regan and his team in their enthusiasm for the Bunratty project, 'which it is hoped will become a major tourist attraction', their first report to the Minister for Industry and Commerce stated. 'It was in our Sales and Catering days that Gort turned up and proposed first of all to rehabilitate Bunratty,' Peter Donnelly, with responsibility for development promotion in O'Regan's team, recalled in 1994. 'We discussed it an awful lot.... As soon as O'Regan heard that the castle was being restored he had banquets in mind. I remember pulling his leg that we'd have him there in the short trousers and long stockings. Everything went ahead from that – the whole thing was being discussed and teased out.'

Various opinions were to be voiced, as will be seen, as to who first hit upon the idea of mediaeval banquets; but O'Regan's enthusiasm from his first meeting with Gort for the project of restoration is well attested. 'As well as being Comptroller of Sales and Catering he was chairman of Bord Fáilte,' said Christy Lynch, 'so he was sort of now trying to dovetail funds from Bord Fáilte and from the Office of Public Works and Lord Gort... . I was given the title of Special Projects Manager to try and set up new projects with a view to increasing tourism in the area and one of the projects turned out to be Bunratty. I was acting as liaison person between Lord Gort, the Office of Public Works and our own company. And it worked very well, I must say, in the early, formative years.'

As O'Regan and his colleagues debated, the complex task of reconstruction proceeded. 'Restoring Bunratty Castle, Co. Clare, solving the gigantic jigsaw of its scattered stones, and cutting away the anachronistic modern structures that were imposed upon the original fabric, are nine men from the Board of Works,' the *Irish Independent* wrote. 'Expert work over the past 14 months has stripped the Castle of some of its more modern 'trimmings'... . Remains of the old RIC barracks burned down during the Troubles have now been removed.'

It must be remembered that the conditions under which this daunting programme of conservation and restoration was undertaken differed vastly from those which might be encountered today. There was no master plan or fixed timetable, such as would now be a prerequisite. A further complicating factor was that, though the Office of Public Works in the person of Le Clerc was nominally in charge, Gort and Hunt had their own firm ideas as to what should be done and were not loth to insist on them. The initial funding was minimal, certainly insufficient to complete the task in its entirety, and new sources of finance had to be sought out and negotiated as work proceeded. The OPW foreman, Thomas Kavanagh, had no permanent, dedicated workforce but had to rely on locally-recruited direct labour. All these factors were to combine with the uncertainties of the weather and the difficulty in acquiring suitable materials to ensure that the undertaking proceeded both erratically and spasmodically, and with no certainty that it would ever be fully realised. Moreover, in spite of a succession of surveys and recommendations over the years, it was not until work was actually under way that the daunting complexities of what lay ahead were to become apparent.

'The work had a great deal of the interest of a detective story,'

Le Clerc told the Thomond Archaeological Society, 'and this helped to keep us all going when difficulties of one kind and another impeded the smooth running of the work.' And he reiterated the guiding philosophy: 'Ideally the new work necessary for preservation should not be visible, but in restoration this is not possible, of course, and the best one can do is to ensure that the new work is not too conspicuous. An architect who visited the castle at a time when the work was half finished unintentionally paid us the compliment of saying that as far as he could see we had not done very much to it in all the time we had been working on it. A big Dublin contractor... looked up at the roof and said what a fine roof it was after all these centuries!'

In implementing his philosophy Percy Le Clerc was most fortunate in his patron, Lord Gort. 'I was particularly grateful to him during the many discussion we had as the work proceeded,' he admitted to the Thomond society, 'for the way he left me and my staff free to carry out the restoration strictly in accordance with the clues we found; the result was that the work of restoration did not disturb a single stone of the original fifteenth-century fabric.' (A claim not entirely sustained by the evidence.) 'In each part of the building,' he explained in 1979, 'the first operation was the careful removal of the later work to lay bare the original fifteenth-century fabric; this operation could be done with precision because the quality of the fifteenth-century work was easily distinguished from later work: the mortar was very hard and the dressed stones had a characteristic form of fine tooling.' The most notable later additions that were retained were the South Solar of *c* 1580 with its renaissance fireplace and the decorative plasterwork, *c* 1600, in the Great Hall chapel and elsewhere.

If Gort was standing back from any controversy over the work itself (and again, as it transpired, this was not to continue to be wholly the case), he was consistently unstinting in his practical enthusiasm. In August 1957 Thomas Kavanagh's workmen were involved in demolishing walls at Lough Cutra to provide stone for use in the reconstruction and drawing it to the site with the Gort estate tractor and trailer; and he was constantly in pursuit of suitable artefacts to furnish the building when completed. 'It looks to me as if we are going to have a wonderful castle when it is done,' he wrote to Le Clerc on 8 July 1957. 'I have found another early oak cabinet and I believe we may have enough now. I saw the door for the secret stair in the chapel and it has cleaned up very well... . Could we start and send some furniture across when we send some more oak? It is all early furniture and will not suffer in transport.'

Le Clerc had designed a new roof for the Great Hall based on that of the Plunkett castle at Dunsoghly, County Dublin – the sole surviving Irish example from the period – and Gort had been shipping timber for its construction both from Lough Cutra and from Hamsterley Hall. Its fabrication fascinated Joe McElgunn: 'It was all worked, in actual fact, with green timber and it ruined the carpenters' tools. It became dark and rusty and discoloured but the theory was that as the timbers shrank the whole thing kind of shrank in a unit and balanced out so that there was no great distortion and that the thing sat snug on the wallplates – which is as it turned out. I saw it put together in the Great Hall and it looked fantastic.'

'All joints are secured with oak pegs,' Le Clerc wrote. 'It was

*Moulds being utilised to reproduce stone dressing*

common practice in the middle ages to use unseasoned oak for carpentry; large roof timbers do not warp very much, but such distortion as does occur tightens the joints and gives character to the carpentry.'

Gort at this period was visiting the castle from England at approximately fortnightly intervals. His far-flung business affairs, however, continued to demand his attention and on 8 August 1957 he was writing from the Fort Garry Hotel in Winnepeg: 'Dear Le Clerc, I am sending you a line from this side of the Atlantic to say how pleased I was with the way Bunratty looked and also to say what an improvement the parapets are. I feel happier now that I can walk on the floor of the South Solar. My wife and Hunt and Walford the Gort lawyer are arranging about the scheduling of the furniture... . I think the Great Hall roof you designed looks very good.'

The 'parapets' to which Gort was referring were the entirely new crenellations which Le Clerc had 'reconstructed' and which were to arouse perhaps more controversy in archaeological and

*At work on the NE tower, July 1957*

conservation circles than any other facet of the restoration. They were modelled on those of Quin Abbey, County Clare, founded by Mac Con Macnamara in 1433 and incorporating an earlier castle of Thomas de Clare; on Jerpoint Abbey, County Kilkenny, and particularly on those of the small tower house at Clara in the same county. 'Obviously we had no evidence for the crenellations,' Le Clerc admitted in 1994, and though, as he insisted, they represent a distinctively Irish treatment of castle battlements their authenticity, as distinct from their contribution to the total effect, must remain open to question. This feature apart, there was no need, he claimed, for 'inspired' guesswork: the slope of the roof was indicated by the architecture, for example, as was the internal layout, though 'some of the things were pretty slender. There was one thing that turned up,' he remembered. 'This was the royal coat of arms – a fifteenth-century one – which had been broken. Carved in limestone. Gort was afraid to put it up because he didn't want to hurt nationalist feelings. I thought this was going a bit far – people in the IRA wouldn't recognise the lions and fleur-de-lis. I often wondered what became of those pieces.'

Gort's reservations, given the temper of the times, were probably justified. On 1 January 1957 Sean South and Fergal O'Hanlon had been killed in an IRA attack on the Brookeborough police barracks in County Fermanagh and on 8 July the Irish government invoked the Offences Against the State Act of 1940 to deal with the IRA campaign in the North of Ireland. At local level, too, the Bunratty restoration aroused from the outset the hostility of those who felt it represented the resurrection of an alien presence, awakening bitter memories of battles not so long ago. One of the later additions to the castle which disappeared without trace in the reconstruction was the police barracks.

'My father used to go down to that barrack quite often to play cards with the police,' said Paddy Corbett, 'and the man in charge there was a Sergeant Curtin – this would have been in 1920. Like all other policemen he used to patrol on his bicycle. But one particular day Curtin took off on his bicycle down the main road to Limerick and he took the first turn on the left up towards Cratloe. And he was shot from behind the ditch by the

IRA. He was knocked off his bicycle but he wasn't mortally wounded. The gunmen came out from behind the ditch and he asked for a priest. "I'll give you a priest," said the leader, and shot him in the head.'

The expenditure on the project, a sum substantially augmented by local rumour, was also to encounter its critics. The *Limerick Leader* was moved to complain on 1 March 1958 at the state of the playground in the city's Model Schools: 'The surface, loose, rough gravel, is most dangerous from the point of view of young children should they fall during periods of recreation... . Could not the Board of Works spare a little money to have the enclosure covered with asphalt? This should be possible, seeing that thousands of pounds may be spent on the restoration of a twelfth century castle in order to make it an international museum of some sort.' With the inauguration of the mediaeval banquets the begrudgers – now ranging over a much wider spectrum – were to find a new focus for their disapprobation.

If Le Clerc felt obliged to resort to conjectural restoration in the matter of the crenellations, Gort was offered little choice when it came to authentic furniture and furnishings – there was

*The new crenellations, November 1957*

just nothing available of proven Irish provenance from the period of the Great Earl. This, of course, left him with a clear field and he approached the task with what could only be described as single-minded ruthlessness. The locating, shipping and installing of suitable artefacts closely involved Christy Lynch, who developed a strong relationship with both Lord and Lady Gort and found Hamsterley Hall 'like an Aladdin's Cave with lovely things, early things... . They lived within that period and felt no difficulty, really, in using utensils or furniture of the period. They lived like that.' Lynch began to share their enthusiasm and to learn from them: 'They were a marvellous couple to know and they spoke of the bits and pieces with great affection. They had quite a lot of things in museums in England and in Winnepeg. I know that their Saint George and the Dragon – it's a wood carving in the Great Hall – was in the Winnepeg museum and Lady Gort decided that she'd like it for Bunratty, so she made approaches to the curator and she always tells the story that he parted with it with a bleeding heart.'

The heavier items were shipped to Limerick on the vessels of the Limerick Steamship Company ('They're gone from it now,' said Joe McElgunn, 'but they were a great asset in having furniture transferred from Lord Gort's place into Limerick Dock') and brought from there by road. 'There was always great excitement when Salkeld's truck would arrive here,' Tom Sheedy remembered, 'and great excitement getting the furniture up into the castle.'

The acquisition and transportation of the twenty-two-foot table for the Great Hall was typical of the way Gort operated. 'I went over with Lord Gort,' Christy Lynch recalled, 'because he had seen that table advertised by a Lady Baillie, who owned Leeds Castle, a beautiful moated castle. But we went to see the table and I think we bought it for something like £600 or £700.[2] It must be ten times that value now. But I was saddled with the job of getting the table from Leeds to Bunratty and the leaf is all in one piece. The frame came dowelled and just came asunder. But to get the leaf out of the castle we had to get it out of one of the windows and drop it into the moat and then fish it out of there. I was saying aspirations that it wouldn't crack when it hit the water, but it didn't. So it eventually arrived in Bunratty and he was very pleased with it. But he used to bring things (and I would say that a lot of the stuff he brought he wouldn't get an export licence for): he used to smuggle them, really, out of England. I remember meeting him at Shannon and he had this sack, an ordinary coarse sugar sack with him up on his back coming off the aeroplane. So I asked him what was in the bag and he put his hand up to his mouth and said, "It's very good!" He did smuggle this particular object out and apparently it had the coat of arms of Richard II.'

'Gort would get off the plane bringing in a mediaeval manuscript on his back,' Marcus Ó hEochaidh remembered, 'and coming through customs with the knapsack like a tramp almost. I said to him, "You're robbing Canada: Canada has very little heritage. We have plenty of heritage here." "Ah," he said, "we'll do something else for Canada." He saw nothing wrong, wherever he got it [in appropriating it] for his particular pet scheme here.'

For Pa Crowe the unconventional furnishing of Bunratty also proved to be a learning process. 'All the furniture was coming in crates. Some of the windows was in on a temporary basis and the mullions at the centre I had to take out. The majority of the furniture was all morticed and dowelled, and I was involved in putting it together.' He was assisted by John Hunt's carpenter from Dublin, 'a fantastic carpenter by the name of Sam Waters. We would work hand in hand. He would go home at the weekend but I kept going all the time.' As he worked, said Crowe, 'John Hunt was giving me all the history of it. I didn't know anything about furniture but it was creeping into me and I compiled a history of the castle unknownst to myself' – which, with the work completed and visitors arriving, he was to put to good use. 'I took a bit of pride in being able to tell them that a carving came from Germany and give them the background and history of it.'

For all his idiosyncratic stratagems, Gort was keeping a beady eye on outgoings. 'We have some big oak at Lough Cutra now so we need not skimp the sizes of timber for the North Solar roof as it is only the sawing cost we need to consider,' he informed Le Clerc on 16 September 1957. On the distinctively contemporary aspects of the enterprise: 'Hunt is still abroad,' he told Le Clerc on the 27th, 'and I wrote him two letters about Bunratty and in one I asked him to suggest to you that the large break through going to the SW tower at level one below the Great Hall might have a thin outside wall when rebuilt and that a bath room and lavatory might be put in without any vandalism and that guests if they must take a bath go here to do it so as not to spoil the mediaeval architecture elsewhere. I recognise that people who want a bath must be treated with some consideration. Visitors who just want to go to the lavatory will be given a chance in the ladies or gents north end paved hall level and they can do it in mediaeval splendour with WOODEN or stone seats.'

Le Clerc's reply, on 3 October, registered some impatience with the whole idea: 'I don't see what they want with a bathroom in a castle – nobody of the bathing classes will ever be here for more than a few weeks at a time', but then he had matters of more immediate import on his mind. First was the good news: 'I was down at Bunratty last week. You will be glad to hear that, having taken down the vault between the N towers, we have found the sockets of the drawbridge. They are on each side of the chamfered doorway (that was supressed to insert the moulded doorway) of which, you remember, only one jamb remained in situ; the worn threshold of this doorway remains undisturbed and at each end, below it, projected two large corbel stones with flat tops and 45° chamfers underneath; on the inner sides of each are large round socket holes that can only indicate a drawbridge. This is the only known occurrence of a drawbridge of this date so far. We shall have to find a home for the moulded doorway.' Then the bad news: 'The Board will not agree to do more work than would have been necessary to preserve the castle as a ruin.' Le Clerc suggested to Gort that he approach Bord Fáilte: 'Hunt will do this for you I expect.'

While negotiations were set in train the work continued, with Gort delving ever deeper into his store of mediaeval miscellanea. 'I am going over my stained glass panels', he wrote on 5 October from Hamstersley Hall (his syntax falling victim to his enthusiasm), 'and I find I have 3 dozen here some of them quite good ones and I have some more in London perhaps a dozen or more and a lot of which some are old, armorial ones and I will try & sort these out... .'

On the site the weather had deteriorated, and it was very wet and cold. Thomas Kavanagh had to install temporary high-powered lighting in the Great Hall, Paved Hall and basement, as he

*Pa Crowe at work in the castle, 1961*

reported on the 31st, 'to enable inside work to proceed during the evenings'. Meanwhile, Le Clerc was still concerned with identifying pieces of the jigsaw in the light of new discoveries. On 1 November he reported to Gort, 'I examined the south window of the Great Hall and it now seems certain that the tracery at the head is an insertion. Since the plasterwork went across it on the inside it must have been inserted not later than the early 17th century and therefore it is doubtful whether we should move it; if we did decide to move it it would only be to re-use it for the window of the Paved Hall. We are checking whether the moulded "doorway" could not by any chance have been the square external surround to the window of the Paved Hall; it seems very high for a doorway, but the mouldings are unusual for a window... . We found a fine chute about 2' 6" square leading from the little chamber behind the Paved Hall fireplace down to the vaulted basement. At the top of the chute, level with the floor of the little chamber, was a trap-door and the two carved stone sockets for it remain. This will provide a convenient means of bringing up fuel and could even accommodate a service lift. We found a small fragment of blue and white pottery, parts of broken glass flagons and a diamond pane of window glass in the debris.'

Gort arrived on a visit three days later and on his return to Hamsterley wrote to assure Le Clerc, 'Have just heard that the further £2000 will be all right.' He had stepped into the financial breach. He was also contemplating a role for 'a very good Flemish shutter with very good ironwork... this can be opened for Chamber Music or Jazz music in accordance with the taste and nationality of those being fed.' It is clear that the idea of the banquet, or at least of a meal with some kind of entertainment, had already taken root.

'Everybody began to see possibilities then,' said Le Clerc; but the initial approach was to something 'more like a small restaurant – that was the nucleus of it and then it developed into your banquets eventually'. At this stage, however, no one could envisage that the idea would grow to the extent it did. 'I used to be trying to persuade Gort to buy Durty Nellie's because, I said,

"You know people would want something to eat... it would be a great asset to the place." Later, 'I remember Christy and me working on a plan to purchase Durty Nellie's,' said Tom Sheedy; 'if ten people went in there, there wasn't room to swing a cat... to purchase the creamery and to purchase Bunratty Castle Hotel... and to purchase the post office which is now a souvenir shop across the road.'

Earlier, Brendan O'Regan had had the same idea with regard to Durty Nellie's, but the responsible government department of the day did not look favourably on the Shannon Free Airport Development Company, a state-sponsored body as constituted, engaging in the private sector pub trade. With the advent of a more market-orientated political culture, however, a pub, 'P. Macnamara & Son', was to open in later years as one of the features of the Folk Park which not only catered for visitors but, after visiting hours, admitted local drinkers through a special entrance: a case of illusion transmogrified into reality.

In the castle itself, as the year 1957 drew to a close, illusion was, on the contrary, beginning to impinge upon the practical problems of reconstituting the fabric of the building. In a letter to Le Clerc of 14 November, after a discussion as to the positioning of the tryptich in the chapel ('It should go on the E end altar for several reasons, one reason is that it will look wonderfull [sic] through the Great Hall opening'), Gort continues: 'The show dungeons can be in the S towers. I have a few horror pictures for these and perhaps an iron grille in the floor [of the] SW tower instead of a trap door.' From the outset he had planned accommodation for himself and Lady Gort for use in the course of their regular visits, accommodation which he intended to furnish to the same authentic standards as the rest of the restored Bunratty. 'I expect to exchange a horse & also a bishop both wooden ones of course,' he explained in the same letter, 'for a picture of Adam & Eve in Natural Costume of the period, fig leaves, very good & nothing wrong with it but the YMCA [Young Men's Christian Association] would not go out of their way to hang it up. This would help make a very Good Adam & Eve bedroom off the N.

Solar. I will be able to furnish what is called my suite very well and quite up to the standard of the extinct Princes of Thomond.'

Le Clerc was still, however, immersed in the solution of the jigsaw puzzle, as he told Gort on 23 November. 'McCarthy and Clark[3] are both down this week gathering clues and drawing a reconstruction of the entrance lobby. Their researches will help us to come to some finality about this problem. I don't so much object to the idea of a 17th century entrance to the Paved Hall, because the fireplace and floor are both fairly strikingly of that period; but I do fear that the scale and character of it may spoil the visitors' first impression on entering the castle.' On the matter of the east window in the chapel, which had proved a bone of contention, he was, however, prepared to be accommodating. 'I agree with all you say,' he reassured Gort, 'but I fear that not to put in a wider window will antagonise Hunt, which you may prefer to avoid... . I feel that, having those awful vaults taken away with such great advantage to the whole appearance of the castle and with the additional and unexpected advantage of finding the Drawbridge, it seems that the window is a small concession for the sake of peace.' There followed a small dash of cold water: 'I cannot get involved too deeply in Tower C and the North Solar in case we should run out of money and be unable to finish what we have started.'

The question of finance still loomed large, complicated by Gort's vagueness regarding his financial affairs. 'I had no idea whether the Office of Public Works still held a balance of his money in hand or not,' his solicitor, G. H. Walford, wrote to the architect on 3 December. The uncertainties were creating difficulties for Thomas Kavanagh, who had had to suspend work on some of the windows on account of the weather: 'I am fortunate enough to have six good masons on the job. If I cannot provide work for the wet days the job will lose its attractions for the masons, and they will seek employment where they can obtain full time work.'

'They seemed to have a superb group of masons,' Joe McElgunn confirmed. 'Later on there was a lot of building going on by Shannon Development in the industrial estate and Percy

Le Clerc was very annoyed about this, because some of his best masons were being stolen away because they would get more money block laying, building factories.'

'An acute labour shortage is developing here,' Kavanagh was to report to Le Clerc on 12 May 1958. 'Large contracts are opening up at Shannon. The new highway from Shannon to Limerick has commenced, jet fuel storage depots are being erected by the various oil companies.' Wage rates were higher than at Bunratty and there was unlimited overtime: his best labourers had already gone and the three remaining expected to follow them. 'What a pity,' he concluded, 'we couldn't have kept going while conditions were in our favour.'

'The cost of running this job is £200 per week,' the clerk of works had reported to Le Clerc on the previous 17 December, estimating that enough money remained for three weeks' employment. Expenditure of a further £1,500 was approved on 1 January 1958, but on 18 March Gordon Clark advised that Bord Fáilte would not be able to finance the restoration of the North Solar. They would, however, be prepared to help with the electrics.

On 15 May the Archaeological Officer of Bord Fáilte, Kevin Barry, suggested to Gort that a trust, already discussed with Hunt, should be set up to ensure the continuity of the castle and its contents as a period museum. 'Crises are constantly arising at Bunratty,' the letter concluded, 'and I understand that funds are running dangerously low and that if something is not decided, work may have to close down in a few weeks.' Gort and Walford agreed to travel to Dublin to discuss the idea.

On 24 April, Kevin Barry, John Hunt and Joe McElgunn had visited the site to assess what would be required to complete the project. It was concluded that a sum of £10,882 would be adequate, and that this would also provide catering facilities and a car park. A month later, however – on 25 May – E. K. McCarthy, Le Clerc's assistant, gave Gort the bad news that work would have to cease within ten days unless £500 could be assured to cover items essential to the security of the castle. Gort replied with some impatience four days later that 'Hunt said quite definitely that there was more money coming. Now he says

*The highest point to date: working on the chimney of the
NW tower, August 1957*

on the phone that the board [Bord Fáilte] are only waiting for me to sign the schedule of furniture to be dedicated for the castle & this I will do & would have done so anytime during the last 12 months as I promised.' Somebody, he clearly suspected, was playing a game of financial passing-the-parcel.

Bord Fáilte, as promised, came up with the money for the electrics, but on 6 June Le Clerc informed Kevin Barry he had diverted it to work on the Paved Hall. One reason for the board's dragging its feet in the matter of funding would seem to have involved the acquisition of further land and the apportioning of revenues. Gort had, in the mean time, once more retired to Winnepeg, from where on 17 June he wrote to Le Clerc: 'I had a day with Mr Kavanagh after they [Walford and his wife] flew back to London and he showed me a well of which I had no knowledge near the Creamery which could be used by arrangement with Russell and it looks to be as if we would have to buy him out now the Tourist Board are not going to, I mean as regards the 18 acres in question.' He continued, 'We arranged, as you know, for 5 years' revenue to go back to the Tourist Board after expenses and I am inclined to think that this revenue will be bigger than was suggested... I would like to get the north solar roof on soon even if no more and the n.w. staircase completed so that visitors can go up one stair and down the other.' On 3 July a letter from Walford to Kevin Barry confirmed that Lord Gort was prepared to agree that all monies received should '1, discharge all outgoings and 2, be spent on the castle', subject to a review after five years.

There matters were to rest for another four months, during which time Le Clerc and Kavanagh were able to keep the work 'ticking over', as he told Gort on 21 October. The latter's enthusiasm for his self-imposed task had remained, nevertheless, at a high level. 'I think the job is coming on wonderfully,' he had told Le Clerc the previous January, 'and when finished it will take some beating in early Castles unless you go to France or Germany.' Meanwhile he was pursuing further artefacts, some of which at least were to involve compromises with authenticity. 'Crowther [a dealer] has some wonderful armorial shields blank so we can paint what we want 5 of them for the Great Hall which I hope to buy and we can make another 7 somehow in carved oak or composition. Our gardener is a sort of carpenter & I think I can get him to make them.' 'There is almost no hope of getting any more old Great Hall figures,' he wrote in October. 'Could we get what Canadians call a wood butcher to carve some as they are not great works of art but look wonderfull [*sic*] when up in the roof.'

Le Clerc, far from enthused by these reach-me-down suggestions, was given further cause for concern when on 20 May Gort confessed, 'I have been rather a vandal in cutting up some circa 1550 to 1600 stained glass for Hunt's 3 light chapel window [Hunt had won that argument] but it will look very good I hope.' He had also supplied some white window glass which had failed to meet with Le Clerc's approval. The latter suggested substituting old crown glass, but, 'The only large lot of crown glass I know of at present,' Gort responded on 23 October, 'is in old houses upstream from Quebec, Canada & to get this is not a practical proposition... [and] modern crown glass is no better than what we have.'

'I cannot regard the present glass as being reasonably satisfactory,' Le Clerc protested. 'After everyone's efforts and expense in the venture, so far attended with a fair measure of general success, it would be disappointing to have to invite the criticism "if this is the standard of restoration that they have set themselves, we need not take any of it very seriously".'

Gort remained unrepentant. 'I have been to the University here [Newcastle],' he wrote on 28 October, 'as I know the art Professor well & they will carve us 2 more young Ladies to complete the set of 8 Young Ladies for the roof & they will do them in oak... perhaps Kavanagh could tie a label round one of the Young Ladies & send it back here & I will give the University the oak & they can get started.' This was done, and on 15 November he confirmed that 'one young Lady has arrived at Liverpool waiting to get through the Customs and immigration. I have a lot of forms to fill in asking if she is of English origin & whether a citizen of the British Empire.'

In spite of all the impediments, things were taking shape. 'The tapestries look fine in position and the pieces of furniture are already giving the place an inhabited feeling,' wrote Le Clerc. The tapestries were, Pa Crowe remembered, 'the big job. All I had was a ladder, and trying to put a tapestry thirty-five-feet long up on the wall I had no help.' He had to plug the wall, put a slate lath along it and then put on the tapestry to fit; and 'when that would be up John Hunt might say, "That's lovely, Pa, but would you ever drop it six inches." In my case,' he admitted, 'it was more strength than skill I found was required. A lot of it was done very amateurish – you couldn't get a scaffolding crowd to come in – you had to erect a pulley yourself.'

The financial situation, however, remained unclear. 'I seem to get no replies from Hunt,' Gort complained on 29 October; 'perhaps he has lost interest.' He planned to stop over in Shannon on 24 November en route to Chicago and told Le Clerc, hopefully, on the 8th, 'We are one step further forward with the Tourist Board.'

In the mean time Thomas Kavanagh had picked up a bit of local gossip. 'Mr Russell let it be known locally,' he informed his boss, 'that Bord Fáilte has purchased from him an area of land adjoining the Castle for the erection of Hostels for Air Passenger accommodation... . If true [it wasn't] it is very interesting as the area involved contains an area which is bounded by a very fine stone wall and the stone is the same type as the Castle.' Kavanagh's practiced eye saw this as a good source of material when building, which had been suspended, was resumed; his only other source was 'a burnt out composite brick and stone structure near Crusheen'.

It was the nascent Shannon Development, in the person of Brendan O'Regan, who had in fact acquired the site. 'I bought the land nearest to the castle with the idea of getting a motel,' he explained. 'After that 1950 visit I made to America I was convinced that motels were the thing of the future and that we needed to get at least one built in Ireland, and I felt here was the place for it. I didn't have the authority to engage in this kind of work, but I bought the piece of land anyway and we sent Joe McElgunn and I think Jack [J. C.] Lynch to America to see if we could get an investment in a motel. And we got Andy Devane to do a plan. We very shortly after that got Albert McCarthy who came down, looked at the site and said, "I'll do it." Only fourteen rooms to it at that stage.' The hotel (the idea of a motel was dropped) became the Shannon Shamrock and opened in 1959. O'Regan remembered, 'As I was going through the tap room of my father's pub in Sixmilebridge on one occasion, I heard two local men saying, "Bunratty – a hotel in Bunratty: did you every hear anything more ridiculous?" And I would say the restoration of the ruin would locally have got the same kind of treatment for a long time.'

The plans so far proposed for the opening of the castle to the public as a museum included the appointment of John Hunt as curator and the provision of modern living accommodation to be placed at his disposal – an exercise in anachronism located in the South Solar which was not, of course, to be on view to visitors. In his letter to Brendan O'Regan of 4 November 1958 already quoted, Hunt dealt with the expenses likely to arise in running Bunratty: a caretaker and wife; fire and electricity both for caretaker and castle. ('Gort intends to supply timber from Lough Cutra free, the only expense being the cartage. As the castle is not intended to be opened in the evenings except on special occasions, this charge should not be very high. If we cannot afford electric heating in cold weather this will have to be curtailed.') There would also be insurance, and local rates if applicable. In the matter of his own outgoings, he wrote, 'I have so far paid all my own expenses entirely and shall be put to heavy cost in doing up my own quarters, as I have to do everything to make them habitable, all plumbing ect [sic] and even the plastering of walls and laying of floors. I shall be Curator, and for this of course I shall expect no pay. If you can arrange that I and Putzel can be given some ex officio posts with Shannon Development or the Airport, the travelling would be no hardship and the position with Gort and Board [sic] Fáilte would be eased as Board Fáilte wish the actual director to be a member of your staff. Gort wants me to be the Director which is also the easiest all round.'

Later, he suggested, a gardener and further guides might be

required, also advertising and 'any entertainments and the development of our suggested Elisabethan [sic] meals or parties. I think these should pay for themselves once the necessary equipment is provided.' He told O'Regan he was preparing a guide to sell to visitors, and that he envisaged 'some sort of shop to sell Souvenirs which would also be a source of income'. A handwritten postscript explained that 'I do not intend to spend all my time at Bunratty. I suppose I shall be there for 2 or 3 days at a time or perhaps longer, every fortnight or so, once the place is running smoothly.'

On 8 December 1958 Gordon Clark wrote to Le Clerc with the welcome news that Bord Fáilte was making an additional grant of £6,100. Gort had formally undertaken, should that sum not prove adequate, to complete the works at his own expense. Le Clerc was not overly impressed: the works, he replied, would close down on 3 January unless something tangible was forthcoming before that. On 30 December he reported to his own Board that an agreement had been reached 'on condition the owner shall carry out certain additional works to the satisfaction of Bord Fáilte. We are employed by the owner, not as contractors but simply as paid agents to do, on his behalf, the work he had undertaken to get done.' The financial liability, he emphasised, was his. Work would cease on 3 January, he continued, in accordance with the board's instructions and 'work started at Carrick[4] in order to keep the Clerk of Works fully employed cannot now be suspended.' In any case, he added, full-scale work at Bunratty was not possible at this time of year; he envisaged resuming in March.

One of the principal causes of the delay in agreeing the funding of the work remaining to be done lay in the fact that nothing quite like the Bunratty project had ever been attempted before. Involving as it did three state agencies, each with a different agenda, an owner with little experience of the Irish and their ways and an antiquarian pursuing his own aims, it is not surprising that in the circumstances progress should have been slow. The Board of Works, both officially and in the person of its inspector, saw itself as the body with ultimate responsibility and, therefore, with a pre-emptive role. While work was in progress Brendan O'Regan found himself from time to time welcoming American visitors to Shannon to whom he was anxious to show off the castle. 'With reluctance, Percy Le Clerc issued him with a permit to produce to the foreman on the job or in his absence the man in charge,' said Joe McElgunn. 'The workforce had been told not to discuss any of the restoration work with any visitors. It illustrates the way he played his cards close to his chest, I think.'

O'Regan, of course, saw the castle in terms of the remit he had been given by Sean Lemass to save Shannon airport from the effects of overflying by the new generation of jet aircraft. 'We wanted to convert enough transit traffic to full getting-off traffic so that the jets would have to land or lose business. That was the basic idea.' Bord Fáilte's interests were broader: to them Bunratty, though important in terms of a tourist facility, was only one element in a rapidly developing national structure, and not for the first time in respect of the Shannon enterprise policy, differences were to develop between the new state company and existing bodies such as Bord Fáilte and the Industrial Development Authority. Bord Fáilte, for its part, was quite willing at this stage to delegate the management of the enterprise to O'Regan and his team, but as late as 28 November 1958, J. C. Lynch, its Commercial Manager, was apologising to Gordon Clark: 'It is regrettable that you could not have been made aware earlier that it would not be possible for us to enter into a formal agreement with the owners of the Castle as we are not a corporate body. *This only came to light during discussion last week*' [italics added].

O'Regan, however, was typically ahead of events. On 6 December he wrote to Hunt: 'This is to confirm our understanding that on conclusion of the agreement enabling the airport development authority to act as agents for Bord Fáilte Éireann in the management of Bunratty castle, you are appointed as Director and Mrs Hunt as assistant to represent the development authority in management matters concerning the castle. While a fee will not be attached to the post you will be covered for travelling expenses provided the overall revenue from the castle is sufficient to cover these expenses in addition to those already decided upon. Like you, I feel that once we get over the initial stage in this matter we will succeed in establishing the various understandings necessary to enable the operation to be a successful one.'

On 17 January 1959 Gordon Clark wrote to J. C. Lynch: 'I understand that the SFADA [Authority] will shortly become incorporated. Would you please be good enough to let me know, in due course, when this has taken place... . I understand that when the Company is incorporated, you will, through your own Solicitor, Mr O'Donnell, conclude a Management Agreement with the Trustees of the castle. I take it that this Agreement will be on the lines already drafted by Mr O'Reilly, our Solicitor, and submitted to you. In any event, will you please be good enough to let us have sight of the proposed Agreement in due course, as this will be subject to Bord approval. I also understand that you are the nominee of SFADC [Company – the exact title had not then been agreed] on the Furniture Trust.'

*Modern building on the E side being demolished, August 1957*

As work was proceeding on Bunratty and with the now imminent prospect of its opening as a museum, Lord Gort was becoming increasingly concerned as to its long-term future and in particular that of its valuable contents. With regard to the latter, he and Lady Gort had suggested a Trust, 'a group of people', in Tom Sheedy's words, 'who would be responsible for the care and maintenance of the furniture and add to it or sell it'. It was to be widely representative, with the Gorts' solicitor – first Walford, then Colonel Gillman – as a permanent member with the right to nominate his successor; nominees of both Bord Fáilte and SFADCo and, in course of time, certain individuals in their own right. It was to convene at least once a year and examine all the furniture and artefacts item by item. 'In Lord Gort's day it would go on for two or three days because he would start reminiscing,' Tom Sheedy recalled in 1994. 'In those days,' J. C. Lynch confirmed in the same year, 'it took about three days. The day before yesterday [Lynch, on his retirement from Shannon Development, had become a Trust member in his own right] it took less than three hours. Lord Gort would reminisce about

*Bedding of tiles uncovered in the upper chapel*

every item in the castle: it was a very slow and tedious process, though very interesting in some ways.'

The original Deed of Trust, dated 12 June 1959, listed thirteen entries: '1. Elephant tapestry; 2. 2 16th century Brussels tapestries; 3. 2 Verdure tapestries; 4. 1 English Verdure tapestry; 5. Oak Hutch cupboard; 6. Fragment of Gothic tapestry; 7. 3 pictures; 8. 12 early 16th century cupboards; 9. 2 13th century chests; 10. 2 iron clocks; 11. Gothic carvings; 12. Three tables; 13. 3 oak beds. Total value £12,400.' (One tapestry alone was valued at £2,000.) By 1 October 1963 the inventory had grown to 198 items, including forty from John Hunt, a large grid iron from Commander Russell, the former owner, a Great Irish Elk from Dunraven Estates, and an Armada Table, five paintings of Earls of Thomond, an iron-bound chest and an elk head from Lord Inchiquin.

Four years later, in a memo dated 4 June 1963, Peter Donnelly set out for his colleagues in SFADCo the legal situation with regard to Bunratty as then obtaining:

1.  Bunratty Castle is owned by Lord Gort.
2.  By Deed of Guardianship the Commissioners of Public Works are appointed Guardians of the Castle. The Guardianship Deed is dated November 3rd 1954 under the National Monuments Act 1930. Parties to the Deed are Lough Cutra Estates, Richard Henry Russell, Commissioner of the [sic] Public Works.
3.  Deed of Settlement, July 15th, 1956. By this Deed Lord Gort vested the Castle in John Hunt and Desmond J. O'Malley as Trustees, to hold for the Viscountess Gort for her life, then for Viscountess de l'Isle. Lady Gort thus becomes the beneficial owner of the Castle. Parties to the Deed are John Hunt, Desmond J. O'Malley, Lord Gort.
4.  Deed of Trust, June 12th 1959. By this Deed Lord Gort transferred to Trustees furniture and other items in the Castle, listed in the Schedule to the Deed. Parties to the Deed are Lord Gort, Lady Gort, Bord Fáilte Éireann, the Development Company. The Trustees are Lord Gort, Hugh Walford, K. L. Barry, J. C. Lynch.

5.  Management Agreement, December 31st 1959. By this Agreement the Development Company, with the consent of the Commissioners of Public Works and Bord Fáilte Éireann, became managers of the Castle on behalf of its owners. Parties to the Agreement, Lady Gort, the Development Company and the Furniture Trustees.

6.  The Management Agreement provides that the Company is entitled to sub-let or delegate the powers and rights conferred by the Agreement. The Agreement was in fact entered into by the Development Company in order to facilitate operation of the castle by the Sales and Catering Service.

By the time Pa Crowe got a start at Bunratty in May 1959, work had recommenced following the solution of the financial difficulties and the OPW requirement to further the restoration at Carrick-on-Suir, and most of the major reconstruction was completed. 'There was no doors in the castle only the front door and the basement door. I had to take oak timber, seven by one. 'Twas fierce hard work because it had been dried out – kiln dried. I had to rebate it. They had to be put on irons out into the walls with grooves on them. They'd be crudish kind of doors because I wouldn't be a fully-fledged carpenter. But it suited.'

Some of Crowe's fellow workers, according to Le Clerc, were still under the impression that John Hunt was taking too much credit for his part in the restoration. Knowing that Hunt had a fear of heights they discouraged him from inspecting the work in progress by telling him he would have to climb ladders. He was not inhibited, however, from placing to the best advantage the furniture and artefacts that continued to arrive; though when Tom Sheedy first began to work at the castle a year after the opening in 1960, 'the Main Guard was laid out as it might have been at the time, the Great Hall and the North Solar were furnished, part of the Earl's bedroom, two chapels... I think that was it. That was only about a third of the castle.'

'It is highly improbable that Bunratty Castle, as a showpiece, ever will "pay its way",' a leading article in *The Irish Times* predicted two days after the opening. 'If only three or four of the stately houses of England, with all the resources of publicity at their disposal, fail to do so, what hope is there for an obscure castle on the Shannon?'

## Notes

[1] In 'The Restoration of Bunratty Castle', Instituto Italiano dei Castelli, Roma 1979.

[2] The actual cost was £800 excluding transport.

[3] Kevin McCarthy of the OPW, Le Clerc's assistant, and Gordon Clark of the Technical Department of Bord Fáilte.

[4] The Butler Castle at Carrick-on-Suir, County Tipperary. Conservation work by the OPW started in 1948 and was carried out at intervals until 1960.

# A Mick at the Court of King Arthur

**P**ERCY LE CLERC was not present: he was in Switzerland, on loan and acting as secretary to the International Castles Institute – with its headquarters in Schloss Rapperswill – when Bunratty was formally opened on 28 May 1960 by Erskine Childers, Minister for Transport and Power. There was 'the minimum of fuss', in Joe McElgunn's recollection. However, as Christy Lynch remembered it, 'It really was a gala performance. About four or five hundred people at it. There was mass in the chapel off the Great Hall celebrated by the then Bishop of Killaloe and there was a choir of priests on the dais in the Great Hall singing that lovely plain chant... everybody was in ecstasies about it. I remember Lady Gort saying to me, "You know, if this is the way you operate in the Catholic church, I'm going to change my religion!"'

The mass, celebrated in fact by Fr P. Barry, parish priest of Newmarket-on-Fergus, took place at midday, followed by the official opening an hour later. Amongst those present were people who attracted attention even in far-away Dublin: *The Irish Tatler & Sketch* listing the Honourable Grania O'Brien, Mrs Nora Coleman, Lady Inchiquin, Lord and Lady Adare [*sic*], Kay Petersen of the Anna Livia Boutique, the architect Michael Scott. Also on hand were the film director John Huston, then living in County Galway, and his daughter Angelica; the Limerick novelist

Kate O'Brien; the Earl of Dunraven from Adare; the Countess of Rosse from Birr Castle; Joseph Brennan, Parliamentary Secretary to the Minister for Finance, among others. Following the official ceremonies John Hunt conducted interested parties on a tour of the castle and its furnishings.

He would have begun, as he began his description in the brochure that he wrote shortly afterwards, with the drawbridge, 'evidence for the restoration of which was discovered during the recent works', leading his group into the Main Guard, pointing out the line of demarcation on the floor 'defining the area occupied by the officers at the upper end of the chamber from the general rabble of soldiery and retainers', and drawing attention to Gort's furnishings: a 16th century tapestry, woven at Oudenarde in Belgium, on the west wall; an elaborately carved dower cupboard, Westphalian and mid-16th century, ornamented with religious scenes. The group moved to the great limestone chimney-piece on the east wall, 'which dates from the late 16th century and is one of the Great Earl's "improvements", replacing the original 15th century fireplaces, part of the hood of which you can see, there, above the present lintel'.

And, after admiring the armour and crossbows on the walls, the massive 17th-century table, Hunt would have led the way up the main stair and into the Great Hall, which must have astonished those in the party seeing it for the first time. He would have worked clockwise round the vast chamber, pointing out the fine oak Rhenish carving of the conversion of St Hubert; the early 16th-century crucifix; the beautiful Brussels tapestry from the same century; the rare late 12th-century long chest, the equally rare Gothic iron clock next to the kitchen door...

And so on to the Chapel, with its finely decorated plaster ceiling, 'evidently of the late 16th-century and one of the Great Earl's modifications of the castle' (Hunt would not have resisted the opportunities to draw attention to those features which had survived Le Clerc's reductionist concept); up the small stair in the western wall for a close look at one of the fourteen garderobes; a glance at the 16th- and 17th-century implements in the kitchen, unusual in the context as being of Irish provenance; and then to the Earl's private apartments, the great North Solar with its roof restored with Loch Cutra and Hamsterley Hall timbers. It is unlikely that the curious would have been offered access to their South Solar counterpart, 'a series of three rooms with a wonderful southern aspect, evidently used by some important member of the family, or by favoured guests. They are now occupied by the curator and used as offices'.

There was, of course, much, much more – and Hunt, with further groups waiting for the grand tour, would have had to have been selective. From it all, however, would have emerged the awesome scale and dimension of what had been undertaken and achieved: the vast size of Bunratty, the bewildering complexity of halls, rooms and chapels, of kitchens and dungeons and garderobes, brought home by the sheer abundance of Lord Gort's priceless artefacts. On every wall, in every window of what had been only three or four years earlier a crumbling ruin, they lent life and that transcendent impression of immediacy that was to be subsequently remarked upon by so many.

And as for that modest man, Lord Gort, in 1937 he had intended to be present at the coronation of King George VI, only to be informed that as an Irish title holder there was no room for him in Westminster Abbey. Now, a quarter of a century later, he confessed to the Irish edition of the London *Daily Mail* that he had refused an invitation to lunch the same day with the king's daughter, Queen Elizabeth, and her husband Prince Phillip in his capacity as a former High Sheriff of County Durham on the occasion of her opening the new town of Peterlee. 'I regret very much that the two events clashed,' he said, 'but this is my life's work.'

The menu for luncheon, to be served in the nearby Shannon Shamrock Hotel, had been the subject of intensive research into dishes appropriate to the period. It read, in part:

### Course I
Mussells, Pettitoes, Soused Trout, Salmon in Verjuice,
Half'd Carp, Tench, Wild Game, Eel, Picked Mushroom,
Beetroot, Cucumbers, French Beans, King's Soup.

*Course II*
Venison Gobbets, Lamb, Broiled Chicken,
Pig in jelly (*Muicfheoil le Ghlothaig*),
Neat's Tongues in Paper (*Teangacha Caorach Paipéirithe*),
Ham, Baked Ox Cheek, Green Peas, Seville Orange Sallet.

*Course III*
Â Sotelte, Black Caps, Gooseberry Fool,
Everlasting Syllabubs (*Suthâin Carraighín*),
Brown Bread Cake.

But the guests were to be deprived of the opportunity of sampling syllabubs made with carrigeen, or seaweed. 'Lady Gort was all set to play hostess at a fifteenth century feast in keeping with her husband's fifteenth century Bunratty castle,' the *Daily Mail* of 30 May reported, 'when the banquet suddenly turned into a barbecue, and switched from a top hotel to an airport garden. "I couldn't have cared if I had been served a boiled egg," joked Lord Gort last night.' Catering workers, members of the Irish Transport & General Workers' Union, had refused to augment

the hotel staff because, they said, it was not a union shop, so the banquet cum barbecue took place instead in an area close to the terminal building at Shannon, the exotic menu replaced by venison (or, some say, roast pig) on a spit. Perhaps because of the day that was in it, both the sequence and location of events remained unclear to at least one individual present.

'The mead was the speciality of the day,' Bill Maxwell, then working as a press and information officer with SFADCo, remembered; but it quickly ran out and was surreptitiously replaced by sherry. And he clearly recalled the roasting of the pig as having taken place in the castle grounds: 'The reception and drinks were at Bunratty, definitely.'

The pig, wherever it may have met its end, has over the intervening years attracted its own corpus of legend. 'I always remember,' claimed Maxwell, 'one of the young students from the Hotel School [at Shannon] manning the rotisserie and at one

Left: *Lord and Lady Gort with Lord Boyne (centre) at a Bunratty banquet, 1965*

Right: *Brendan O'Regan at Bunratty, 1965*

stage Childers came over to him and said, "Well, do you think it's done?" "I don't know," he said, "but I'm fuckin' overdone, I tell you."' Other versions favour Brendan O'Regan as the inno- cent enquirer, but somehow the story chimes more happily with the dry, humourless Cambridge tones of the future President of Ireland. Whatever the truth of it, the subsidence of the planned grand gesture into something approaching farce was not entirely inappropriate to the lengthy and devious process which had resulted in the realisation by five down-to-earth idealists of what had appeared to many as an impractical if not somewhat deranged dream.

On 17 June 1959 Peter Donnelly had written to the Civil Aviation Division of the Department of Transport and Power, one of two government departments responsible for the develop- ment of Shannon, regarding 'a proposal to set up at Bunratty a model folk village which would consist of a reconstructed Irish village and rural dwellings. This proposal has arisen from the renovation of Bunratty Castle. The idea is sponsored by the Trustees of Bunratty Castle and the village is to be built on land owned by the Trustees or which they will acquire. My Company [Shannon Development] is anxious to foster the project and assist the promoters. It is for this reason that we have sought per- mission to remove an abandoned cottage from the proposed housing estate.' The 'housing estate' was the nucleus of Shannon New Town which, from a modest beginning in the 1960s with a block of flats on Drumgeely Hill built for employees of the new industries setting up in the duty free zone, was to grow to become Ireland's first substantial new urban community in mod- ern times. The Minister, Erskine Childers, let it be known ten days after the request that he had no objection to the model folk village proposal.

'I don't know where I got the idea in regard to the cottages,' O'Regan admitted. 'I suspect that I got it from John Hunt, and I certainly got encouragement from Childers about it. Maybe I got it from [the architect] Andy Devane – I really don't know. Even while the hotel was being built I wanted to get one cottage built

– just one cottage – as an example of what a traditional Irish cottage might be... . Again money was a difficulty but I spoke to [Albert] McCarthy about it. He said, "How much do you want?" "A thousand pounds," I said. It was very near the hotel and people in the hotel could see it, so he gave me the thousand pounds and that was the first cottage that was put up. They say it was a cottage that was on the site of the runway and so on. I don't think that is so.'

This was another Bunratty legend that was to gain – and retain – popular currency. Pa Crowe remained convinced that 'it stood where the main jet runway in Shannon was being built'. Whatever about the location, the land on which it stood had been owned by John (Red) MacNamara of Drumgeely. 'They were known as Jack Patsies,' said Crowe, 'because there was a lot of MacNamaras in the area; they were all "Macs" to us. They were all nicknamed – that's how you could distinguish the family you were talking about. Mac's place was bought and the house was going to be demolished, but all the local people objected because 'twas a great *cuaird* house. Now a *cuaird* house is where people go in the night to sit down and trace and talk, all the local people. They'd be playing cards – mainly the game they'd be playing is known as 45 – and Mac's was nearly the centre of attraction for everything that happened in Rineanna [the townland which gave its name to Shannon airport]. They were the old aristocracy of the place – everyone was welcome to John Mac's.'

Pa Crowe approached John Jennings, whose firm was building the hotel, and he agreed that when he had finished it he would build a thatched house, if Crowe could get permission. 'So I got onto Mr Lynch, and they bought the house. I was involved in the building – 'twas I got all the material. The reed – I got people down in Caonagh [on the Shannon estuary] to cut it. These people would be part-time fishermen as well and in long parts of the winter they'd be laid off and it was a great source of revenue for them. I came from a thatched house myself, so I knew how they were thatched, where the reed was got, where you'd come by scallops, why there was a flag floor in the house, why the back door was in line with the front one, which would be very bad architectural-wise but when you had big open fires there was a tendency to smoke, so you opened the door at the windy side and that drove the smoke up the chimney. But if you wanted to put cows from the front field to the back it was very appropriate to hunt them across the house, especially if you wanted to impress friends that you had one cow more then they had.'

Like the castle itself, the MacNamara farmhouse was not so much a restoration as a recreation – it remains an open question as to how much of the original building was incorporated into the finished product. According to Joe McElgunn – who also believed it to have stood in the path of the new runway – 'some of the timbers were removed'. The final result, however, was like the castle uncompromisingly authentic in terms of its fabric and furnishings. The Clare farmhouse, the nucleus of what would become the Folk Park, was formally opened simultaneously with Bunratty on 28 May 1960. 'We saw some connection between the Macnamara Castle and the cottage,' said Brendan O'Regan. 'There was a very strong feeling of being Irish in the whole thing that was happening there; and to a certain extent the actual technological thing that was being developed in Shannon, including subsequently the industrial things, created a need for us to counterbalance it with cultural images. And that had, I would say, a lot to do with the emphasis on Bunratty and on the cottages: we were no longer ashamed of the cottage – it was a symbol of Irish endurance.'

For many visitors, however, the Clare farmhouse proved to be a good deal more than a symbol. 'There was a curiosity,' said Joe McElgunn, 'because it wasn't so long ago in their own memories as children – being in the country and being in this type of house with a settle bed, knowing what it was and probably having slept in a settle bed in their youth.'

'There were a lot more interested in the thatched house than there were in the castle,' said Pa Crowe, 'because they could all understand the workings of a thatched house. There was a lot of people who was coming home from America around that time, and they'd come into the castle and say they'd give anything to see the thatched house.' He had to go for the key to the Shannon Shamrock fifteen or twenty times a day. It drew them because 'it was related to their own home they had gone out of fifty or sixty years. You used to see them going to their handbag taking out their handkerchief and wiping their eyes – it was really bringing them back.'

'It was the Lemass era,' said Christy Lynch, 'a very exciting period in Irish life.' Sean Lemass, after years in the wings, had finally assumed centre stage as Taoiseach following the retirement from that office of Eamonn de Valera on 23 June 1959, and it really did seem to many that a new era had dawned. Political isolationism and economic protectionism were to give way to expansion on both fronts: in 1960 the first Irish soldiers to serve with the United Nations were sent to the Congo; Frederick Boland, Ireland's first permanent representative at the UN, was elected president of its General Assembly. Ireland joined the newly formed Organisation for Economic Co-operation and Development and, in the following year, UNESCO. Western Europe, Lemass told the Junior Chambers of Commerce in Shannon in June 1960, was heading for a future of free trade, and Ireland must be prepared to follow. In 1961 the government decided to apply for membership of the European Economic Community.

The policy of industrial protectionism which had been in place since the foundation of the state was about to be superseded by a radical programme for economic development, the brainchild of the Secretary of the Department of Finance, T. K. Whitaker. The key to this policy was the encouragement of foreign investment. 'We can no longer rely for industrial development on extensive tariff and quota protection,' wrote Whitaker. 'Foreign industrialists will bring skills and techniques we need, and continuous widespread publicity abroad is necessary to attract them.' On 1 January 1960 it was reported that the new industrial estate at Shannon expected to create 500 to 600 new jobs. On 3 July a DC 8 of Pan-American Airways became the first airliner to take off from the new Shannon runway, and the first jet to fly from there to the USA on a scheduled flight.

After the disaster years of the 1950s it seemed at last that the tide was turning. Unemployment and emigration fell dramatically (the former in October 1960 down by twenty percent) and Shannon launched a programme to bring back skilled emigrants to ease a labour shortage in the rapidly expanding industrial sector. For those who returned, there were other indications that things were changing for the better, and changing in some cases out of all recognition. On 9 July 1959 Mary Margaret Byrne had become the first Banghárda in a hitherto exclusively male police force; on 31 December 1961 the new national television service put out its first programmes, and on 6 July in the following year introduced the 'Late Late Show' – a programme which was to effect a fundamental change in the social climate in the years that followed. An equally far-reaching change was brought about by the completion of the rural electrification scheme in 1962, which brought rural Ireland irrevocably into the modern era. And if there were those who lamented the eclipsing of what they regarded as traditional values, the great majority turned their eyes in expectation towards the new horizons. From one of the most charismatic of those horizons, President J. F. Kennedy arrived in June 1963 to claim his Irish inheritance and persuade the country that at last it had taken its place among the nations of the world.

For those involved in the promotion of the Shannon enterprise, in which Bunratty was to play a central part, the climate could scarcely have been more propititous, the enthusiasm more infectious. In 1961 Tom Sheedy was still attending the Christian Brothers' school in Limerick and was looking for a summer job. His father, also Tom, was one of the early members of SFADCo and he applied for work at the castle – 'Christy Lynch came and interviewed a troop of us in the hall of the school.' He loved the job from the moment he came out. 'There was something absolutely magic about it. I used to walk out from Limerick to Bunratty on a Sunday, and not only walk out but bring a few of my schoolmates with me.' He was assigned to the small souvenir shop which had been set up in the basement: 'We used to sell a lot of leprechauns, shillelaghs and shamrocks, but Brendan O'Regan never like us to sell these, he felt it was not the image we should project.' He worked with Breda O'Donovan, later one of the entertainers, and he remembered their both waiting to get the results of the Leaving Certificate, 'ringing up our respective schools to find out how we got on'. Young Sheedy's wages as a tour guide were £3 9s. 1d. [£3.45 approx] for a six day week from nine to six with no lunch breaks. It was important, he insisted, that you should make tips. At first he found this very

*Christy Lynch, at the 'Armada' table in the North Solar, 1963*

embarassing, 'but as time went on we would get very clever and rattle money in our pocket just to remind them!'

In the first year that it was opened, Bunratty attracted some 4,600 visitors, most of them Americans induced to break their journey in Ireland (in those innocent days airlines permitted any number of stopovers without penalty as long as there was no backtracking) by Brendan O'Regan's offer of a free day tour. 'They were given a morning tour of the Clare area,' said Joe McElgunn, 'from Limerick to Sixmilebridge, up through Quin, over across to Ennis, saw various things, visited a pub, visited the ruins of Quin Abbey and also had a taste of Guinness, some Irish dancing, and some Irish coffee. And in the evening they had a free fashion show that was put on for them, displaying some of the wares in the airport shop. The following day they had a half-day tour of Limerick city and that completed the stopover.'

It was a bold and original idea, but it failed to take account of the innate human suspicion of anything approaching altruism. 'We thought that if you gave away something for nothing it would market itself,' O'Regan confessed, 'but it didn't go – we only got a few hundred to take the tour over the full summer and we realised then that we had to market it. But we couldn't spend money on marketing giving it away as well, so we charged a price for it then the second year.' It was actually on 1 April 1963 that the free day tour became the one-day tour, priced at US$15 (a dollar above cost) and ending with a banquet at Bunratty.

In his endeavours to promote the tour in America O'Regan had enlisted the support, amongst others, of the journalist Stan Delaplane, who had done much some years before to publicise Irish coffee in his syndicated travel column. In the early days, said O'Regan, 'I acted as courier because I knew the region. I remember on one occasion bringing Delaplane back... . He was on the bus tour and we had a deviation at Cratloe to Gallows Hill. There was a great vista from there and I told him, "We're going to put up the gallows and tell the story of the last man who was hung there for stealing sheep". "Have a man hanging from it all right," he said, "but when they ask you, say he is one of the tourists who didn't buy in the duty free shop after he got his free day." That was the idea, you see.'

The free day, though practically and economically non-viable, had provided the impetus from which expanded tours were to grow and which demanded, in their turn, a more professional approach to tourism promotion. On 6 October 1962 Bill Maxwell was sent to New York to open an office for Shannon Development on Lexington Avenue. Three days later Ray Joyce, who had been working with American Express in Dublin, was appointed Travel Sales Manager at Shannon. At that stage, he remembered, the castle restoration was complete but there was still work to be done in the kitchen area. Banquets had started on an experimental basis, but 'there was no great shape in terms of the entertainment. When I came it had been decided that the thing should be developed to a product standard and that it should be marketed both at home and abroad and should be used as a prime attraction for Shannon airport.'

'The strongest impression made by Bunratty is that it bears no resemblance to a museum,' *The Irish Times* had concluded two days after the opening; and Erskine Childers on that occasion had, in his speech, expressed the hope that the castle would be used 'for the staging of mediaeval banquets and plays by Irish dramatic societies'. If subsequently he was not unwilling to take the credit for having promulgated the banquet idea, there were, as has been seen, other claimants.

'To be an attraction to visitors today a castle must have meaning,' the British journal *The Connoisseur* asserted in 1961; and by then the consensus had already emerged among all those concerned in Bunratty's future that the meaning was to be sought in renewing the life of the castle as much as in restoring its fabric.

'O'Regan came up with this idea of mediaeval banquets,' said Christy Lynch. 'He was talking about it, I'd say, for a year and, you know, nobody was taking him very seriously. So, I remember him saying to Joe McElgunn and myself at a divisional meeting: look, he said, we will have a banquet for ten people there on such a night – which would be a fortnight down the road – and, okay, it's your function to set it up. So Joe McElgunn and I looked at each other. There was no kitchen, there was nothing, there wasn't even running water in the castle at the time. The day dawned anyway, and we brought in tables and linen cloths, set up the whole thing and brought in a few of the Sales and Catering staff who could sing, to perform. Chef Ryan concocted some sort of a meal and I remember McElgunn and myself inside in this little guardroom heating claret on top of a gas tank with a ring on top.' O'Regan, who had bravely invited the journalist Stan Delaplane to participate in the proceedings, found himself dressed in mediaeval costume and wearing a little crown, an actor in his own drama. 'It took off from there,' said Christy Lynch. 'We were a year, possibly two years, tinkering around with it and getting it right.'

Hunt, Gort, Childers, George O'Malley of the Limerick Wine and Food Society – whoever planted the seed it was undoubtedly O'Regan who nourished it. 'Brendan O'Regan has never laid claim to originating anything without inspiration,' Ray Joyce asserted. 'One of his gifts was to recognise it. He had the doggedness to pursue it whereas other people just thought about it. He was the one who made it happen.' As far as the banquets were concerned, Joyce said, 'The original idea that Brendan had was that the castle was now restored... and that it might be a nice thing to hold a state banquet on special occasions. It wasn't originally a commercial concept, but the experiments proved to be so successful.'

Nor was it, it has to be admitted, entirely original. As the idea developed, Peadar Lamb of the Abbey Theatre was asked by Kevin O'Doherty, travel manager of Bord Fáilte, if he would go down to Bunratty to help organise the banquet on a commercial basis. The already-established format, he discovered, 'was a bit of a cog from the Elizabethan banquet in London and there was, in fact, even a record of that knocking around at the time'. This event was then being staged in the basement of the Gore Hotel in Kensington.

'It was started by a girl who had associations with the area and who worked for the BBC,' said J. C. Lynch. 'Her mother lived in Castleconnell. When we started the first banquets she came over here and Brendan got quite a few ideas from that.' Lynch, in common with Ray Joyce and others involved in the project, went to London to see for themselves. 'It was a little bit artificial,' he concluded, 'whereas in Bunratty it's a total atmosphere.' O'Regan emphasised the point that it was unique 'in that it was the first banquet served in a genuine castle. I must recognise that the Gore Hotel in London was perhaps a year ahead of Bunratty – because I went to see it – but we were the first in the world in doing it in a setting of that kind.' Another later pilgrim to Kensington was Lord Gort. 'I picked him up at the airport,' Tom Sheedy remembered, 'and asked him what it was like. "It was quite good," was the reply. "And how did it differ?" "In the Gore Hotel," said Gort, "you can pinch the wenches."'

Nothing like that, of course, was envisaged for Bunratty. ('We couldn't even call our girls wenches because they would get faces on them,' said Sheedy.) O'Regan, for one, was very clear in his mind as to the cultural resonance of the entertainment to be offered. 'I think the purpose of the banquet was that it would have to be genuine or it would be laughed to scorn by the Irish people,' he reflected in 1990. 'When I say genuine, I don't mean that it would be regarded as exactly the way things were done at that time.' He admitted to some extent that there was 'a leg pull going on as it wasn't a serious representation of what the past might have been, when the floor would have been strewn with straw and there would be lots of food lying around.' In terms of the totality of the entertainment offered, however, 'at least it would be seen as not pandering to the kind of rubbish that is sometimes pushed up before tourists; and I think that the essential elements were the authenticity of the castle in which it was being held and the fact that the songs and music related in some way to genuine Irish culture.'

For the trial runs he was obliged, for the moment, to draw upon the artistic abilities available amongst the volunteer banqueters of his Sales and Catering organisation. And, Ray Joyce remembered, 'There were another group of people who were summoned to be an audience – they were known as 'table thumpers' and were also staff members.' 'The Mediaeval dinner at Bunratty is the latest idea of that man of ideas, Mr Brendan O'Regan,' the *Irish Independent* enthused on 14 September 1962, when the press at large was invited to evaluate the experiment, 'and every member of his much and multi-occupied staff helps in its promotion. As chief of the Public Relations office, Miss Maeve Fitzgibbon and her assistants, Mr Bill Maxwell and Mr Tom Tobin, keep a guiding hand and eye on the general plan. Miss Kitty O'Connor, Mr O'Regan's personal secretary, has written most of the script and produces the pageantry with which the dinner is introduced and served. She has a roster of "serving maids" who have already gained some theatre experience from their membership of the Shannon Dramatic Society, which she founded in 1958. Miss Ruth Hill, who plies the mead jug generously, made her first stage appearance with the Shakespearean Society in her native Dublin... She is responsible for display in the Shannon Duty Free shop. Another Dublin girl, Miss Marie

*Erskine Childers, Minister for Transport and Power,*
*takes the chair (R) at a Bunratty banquet, 1963*

Fitzpatrick, exchanges her post at the Shannon Tourist Office with a similar one as courier on the coach tour which precedes the dinner... .The Master of Ceremonies, Mr Jimmy Queally, a member of the Limerick College Players, leads off the revels from the musician's gallery high in the dining hall. The minstrel, Mr Joe Malone of the Development Authority staff, lulls the ear with sweet tunes.'

There was the important consideration, too, of what the diners should ingest in the course of being thus lulled. A lot of research was done on the food, said Ray Joyce. The names of the courses were genuine, but 'they found they couldn't serve mediaeval food, because the way they preserved it was with very strong-tasting spices, which would be totally unacceptable to today's palates'.

'The menu, from soup to sweet, has been devised by Mr William Ryan, head chef at Shannon,' wrote the *Irish Independent*,

*Lord Inchiquin presides at a castle banquet, 1962*

'his source being a 15th century cookery book from which the owner, Dr Robert Wyse Jackson, Bishop of Limerick, allowed him to take copies. The book itself was too precious even for the shortest loan. Mr John Hunt, who planned and supervised the restoration of the Castle and has an apartment there where he and Mrs Hunt stay on their frequent visits to Limerick, has been doing some additional research into mediaeval cookery and Chef Ryan will shortly have new dishes to add to his menus...'

There was a basic necessity, O'Regan recognised, 'to keep the meal reasonably simple but still a good meal.' 'At one time venison was tried out,' Peadar Lamb recalled, 'but it didn't work at all, particularly with Americans. It was a fairly tough type of meat. There were marrowbones used at another stage – I think that lasted for quite some time... and then there was syllabub.' The services of Maura Laverty, writer and well-known culinary expert, were enlisted, and she in turn called in the assistance of the journalist Nuala O'Faolain, then a young student. 'The roots of the idea were very scholarly,' she told *The Irish Times* – anonymously – in 1993. 'They really did want a mediaeval banquet. We came up with about sixty different dishes, but I think they were horrified when they saw what they were.' As for the essential lubrication: 'There was no mead in the country,' said Christy Lynch, 'so I sussed out the monks of Buckfast Abbey. We used to import it in bulk. In the early days we were lacing the wine with brandy, but Customs came down on top of us because we had no licence.'

The first experiments involved no more than about thirty to forty people at three tables, but, said Pa Crowe, 'We had no tables. We had to make stools. I had to get rough timber about nine by two which was similar to ordinary planks and cut a couple of eighteen inch legs and bars off them. At that time we had candles. We used to be burning sods of turf to let people out down the drawbridge – to show them light. We would buy a gallon of paraffin oil and steep the sod of turf in it. We had a few things much like large candlesticks and we would stick them down in the ground and put the sod of turf up on it and light it – that was all my work.' As if that was not enough 'The next thing was, Brendan O'Regan said to me he'd like to see me in costume, so I had to dress up in the pantaloons and jackets and all, and we had an Irish wolfhound. I got the title of Knight of the Castle. I collected the tickets on the drawbridge going in. I was warned: no smile – very stern-looking, to be as a knight would have been with my Irish wolfhound. A lot of people were in dread of their life to pass me. I was a bit worried about that because I would be worried about local people seeing me. One time my father said, "He was all right until he went to Bunratty."'

'You did everything,' Tom Sheedy confirmed; 'you waded in wherever there was a gap. I gradually drifted into working as a butler – I was still working in an office as a clerk.' There was, he said, a great sense of enthusiasm: 'Everyone was prepared to learn. No one had ever done this before.' There were times, however, when the enthusiasm threatened to take the whole enterprise beyond the beyonds.

'Who had turned up in the area and was staying in the Shannon Shamrock but Paul Goldin – the hypnotist', said Peadar Lamb. 'He was talking to Brendan O'Regan and O'Regan was saying, "I wonder now would it be a good idea to invite Paul into one of the dinners and have him produce leprechauns for the guests? Would it be a good idea?"' It would not have been a good idea, for both cultural and legal reasons; and it is a rare example of O'Regan's sure touch betraying him. Fortunately wiser counsels prevailed, and the little people of the barony of Lower Bunratty were left to their own devices.

A castle ghost was also considered in the same context; but the likely reaction of the unsuspecting guests might have considerably outdistanced that of an American lady whom Peadar Lamb vividly remembered. When someone went to tie the little bib round her neck which served instead of a napkin, 'She got a kind of claustrophobia or something and she went, "For God's sake, this goddam thing is choking me – take it away!"'

A much more traumatic occurrence and one which cast a temporary gloom on the otherwise happy sequence of trial banquets was vividly remembered by many of those involved. Judge Gleeson, a well-known Limerick figure with a strong interest in

the local culture, had advised Brendan O'Regan on historical link-
ages and in return was asked would he like to come and see what
was going on. The judge accepted and arrived with either a legal
friend or his daughter – the accounts vary. Something of a poet
and entertainer in his own right (he could sing 'Here's a Health
to You, Father O'Flynn', in Latin and was known locally as the
Bard of Thomond), he was prevailed upon after the meal to recite
some verses of his own on the subject of St Patrick, concluding,
said Peadar Lamb, '"When I go to meet my maker and Saint
Patrick, Great Saint Patrick above" – something like that. He sat
down,' said Lamb, 'and the applause was absolutely fantastic for
him because he did recite extremely well and there was "encore!
encore! encore!"... He was just going to stand up to do an encore
when his head went to one side and came down on the shoulder
of the person next to him.' 'He died right in front of us all,' said
O'Regan. 'I was involved in carrying him out on to the drawbridge and it's almost as if he had planned it, you know. And I
had to go back and tell his wife. "Oh," she said, "he was expecting
it. That's the way he would have wanted it."' 'We carried him
downstairs then,' Lamb continues, 'down underneath the building from the drawbridge and I always remember the top of the
body being cold and when my hand went underneath to lift him
it was still warm and it was a most extraordinary eerie feeling.'

There were no further moves to summon the spirit world to
the Earl of Thomond's table.

The central role of the earl, as with the other ingredients of the
mediaeval evening, evolved from the somewhat hazy basic con-
ception over a number of trial runs. It is now impossible to pin-
point at exactly what stage a notional master of ceremonies was
transmogrified into a reincarnation of My Lord of Thomond.
The idea possibly originated with John Garde, a Cobh-born
South African – 'a big, impressive type of individual', according
to Peadar Lamb, who had returned to Ireland to manage the
new Intercontinental Hotel in Limerick but who had had some
disagreement and left to work for Sales and Catering on tourist
promotion. He became, said Ray Joyce, 'the regular Earl' – and

subsequently married O'Regan's secretary Kitty O'Connor, one of the early scriptwriters.

On 9 September 1962 Betty Jane Robinson, writing in the *Courier Journal* of Louisville, Kentucky, reported a major innovation in the format of the entertainment: 'Just barely down to earth are Merle and Anna Denny of New Albany, who crowned a six week tour of Europe with an Earldom for a day at Bunratty Castle in Ireland.' The tour was a graduation present for their daughter Judy. '"It was all so unexpected," said Anna. "We were there [at Shannon] to go home!" Their day of departure was to have been September 1, time of departure 4.30 pm. But by 4.30 the Dennys... were off on the very first of Shannon's "free-day-in-Ireland" entertainments, royal to a degree... . The Denny's, chosen by Shannon official Brendan O'Regan, were dubbed Earl and Lady of Bunratty, Lords of the Feast, the first to preside over such an event.' This innovation was to stand the test of time and, with the consignment of a less-favoured diner to the dungeons, to prove an effective exercise in instant theatre and audience participation.

'The actual writing of the script, much of which has survived to today, was done by various executives at meetings,' said Ray Joyce in 1994. 'Paul Quigley [then general manager of SFADCo and subsequently O'Regan's successor as chief executive] wrote a lot of the introductory speeches and they're very good – they still stand.' Amongst others who contributed, in addition to Kitty O'Connor, was the Listowel schoolmaster and writer Brian MacMahon. After the first *ad hoc* musical contributions – amongst them Joe Malone singing to his own guitar – it was realised that a more professional approach would be required. 'In the early days,' said Clem O'Sullivan, entertainments manager from 1968, 'you had lads with mandolins pretending they were lutes, and singing lots of rowdy ballads and so on.'

Ray Joyce had a keen interest in music and dramatics – 'I never saw myself as an expert in any field, but it meant that I knew some of the experts in the fields and they couldn't pull the wool over my eyes' – and enlisted the services of Proinnsias Ó Ceallaigh, 'who was a schools' inspector of music and very well known in Dublin – [as director of] the Little Dublin Singers. The commencement of our entertainments was almost hand in hand with the commencement of Jury's Cabaret, and he had the Little Dublin Singers in Jury's.' He was, said Joyce, an expert in the field of traditional music and became involved as a consultant: 'I was very anxious to avoid a situation where we would be having American ballads about Ireland and so on in the castle.'

'We had a number of safeguarding rules in regard to the banquet,' said O'Regan. 'Number one was that it would be prepared for Irish people, not for tourists. Number two was that it would not have the "Mother Machrees", "Irish Eyes are Smiling" – that it would be Irish songs in the Irish language as far as possible. Number three was that its value would be the authentic nature of the castle itself and the authentic nature of those who served, and that those who served would also entertain.'

'In a way Irish music is nearly a stronger link than the language is with the past,' O'Regan was to conclude in 1990. Thirty years earlier it was still the property of the metronomic céilí bands and a small group of cultural traditionalists, and as a mode of popular expression it seemed destined for the dust of the archive. Then, on 30 September 1959, at the Fourth Cork International Film Festival, the documentary on Irish history, *Mise Éire*, was given its première. The music, by Seán Ó Riada, full-blown orchestrations of traditional airs such as 'Róisín Dubh' and 'Sliabh na mBan', captured the public imagination.

'Ó Riada's feat,' wrote the film-maker Louis Marcus, 'was to write a film score in the idiom of an Irish symphonic period that had never happened.' Ó Riada had already established the folk group Ceoltóirí Chualann which provided at least some of the impetus for the founding by Paddy Moloney in 1963 of The Chieftains. '*Mise Éire* excited me,' Moloney reflected in 1995. 'It showed me what you could do with traditional music.' The rest is history.

Ray Joyce and his colleagues and advisers were thus, in hindsight, in the van of the great resurgence of interest in Irish music and its consequent acquisition of an international dimension; though, said Joyce, in the case of Bunratty 'It's more Irish art music – that's because the singers were mostly girls and the appropriate instrument was the harp.' 'Art music' in this sense comprehended the genre of 'Moore's Melodies' and derivatives, together with material from the Irish language tradition already well established in the repertoire.

Between 1880 and 1950, in the view of the composer Gerard Victory, 'Two utterly different traditions existed – often alien and hostile to each other: one was the Gaelic tradition, rooted in a distant past – rejecting harmony and the European academic style in favour of an incomparable melodic richness and decorativeness; the other was the Western European tradition confined to the towns and cities, largely associated with the Anglo-Irish Ascendancy – over-preoccupied with correctness of scholarship, uncertain in its direction, and from 1880 onwards uneasily anxious to make some bridge with the real Irish tradition.' The music for Bunratty represented a similar attempt at bridge-building, with the reinforcement given to the Gaelic element by the new awakening.

The castle entertainment, in Joyce's perception, was also instrumental in developing the national standard of playing of the traditional harp as well as serving as a valuable vocal training ground. 'Many of the girls who have gone on to singing careers have said that they never expected to meet the kind of disciplined singing that was demanded of them.' This was to come. The music featured in the formative stage relied heavily on the home-grown exponents of the popular ballad tradition. 'Dermot Kelly was one of the people who did a lot of the singing at the time,' Peadar Lamb remembered. 'He had a very good ballad voice and he sang extremely well. He had a very good repertoire of Percy French songs... that was the type of song used there. When I was there at that time I used to sing the odd song like "Róisín Dubh" and "Una Bhán" and so on, and later the girls who were there used to sing in unison.' But by this time the Bunratty banquets had passed out of the experimental era into that of commercial reality.

Towards the end of 1962 the organisers felt enough confidence in their nascent product to begin to introduce it both to the press and to a widening invited audience. The reaction of the former group was, predictably, mixed: an impression had been created in certain quarters that, in the words of the columnist 'Mercator' of *The Irish Times*, 'it was a vulgarian show and that the whole affair could be written off as a rather demeaning demonstration of stage Irishism' (his own conclusion was, however, that it was 'a magical experience'). On 22 October the Dublin *Evening Press*, not then known for its concern for happenings beyond the Pale, informed its readers that 'An irresistible tourist (and domestic) attraction is now running through numerous dress rehearsals in Bunratty Castle... . When you go to dinner... the great black oxen of the years retrace their steps. It isn't the 1960s anymore, and you are not a little man in a charcoal grey lounge suit. You are Walter Mitty, day-dreaming again, and you are about to be the guest of the Earl of Thomond. Pick your own rank and title... . The story is all here, in Bunratty, and these gay and light-hearted dinners are touched, for those with even the slightest sense of drama, with a curious sense of reality.'

There were others who took more convincing. 'There was a guy, he was the, what do you call it, of the National Museum' – Joe McElgunn was trying to recall the name of its then Director, A. T. Lucas – 'who said he would never go there, because it was just a bloody gimmick. It was a dreadful thing to do; but afterwards he did come, and apologised for prejudging it, and he found it a very pleasant evening. And you had a lot of the Dublin press... outside the capital, of course, nothing is of any value.' Even amongst the five prime movers in the Bunratty project, the attitude varied. 'Percy Le Clerc was opposed to it too,' said Christy Lynch. 'But what Percy wanted was not to have the banquets in the castle, but to build a banqueting hall. He had found, in the excavation, evidence that there was a banqueting hall in the grounds of the castle and his idea was that it could be got at from the basement where the old police barracks was built on the west side and bring visitors into the castle for a reception, then out to this banqueting hall.'

This was a view echoed by his employers. 'OPW have said more than once that they are not happy with the banquet operation and would like us to consider moving it out of the castle,' said Tom Sheedy. 'There is a foundation in the Rinuccini gardens which Marcus Ó hEochaidh said was an old courthouse or stable or armoury. On that foundation we should rebuild the mediaeval hall that was there.' An architectural model was made, but the idea progressed no further.

John Hunt also had his reservations. 'The banquet hall seated forty and as it happened the coach load was also forty,' said Ray Joyce. 'So that seemed okay. But gradually local people started buying into the banquets and of course local business people found it a magnificent place to entertain. John Hunt was the curator of the castle and he really had a very strong say in what happened there. So that became an area of a little unease. I think the agreement with Hunt was that it would be sixty, but when it went up to eighty I remember meeting him one night and he was saying it looked very crowded. I told him there was a special group there that night and he said, "Every night I come it seems to be a special group" – which was the truth. But he was a most co-operative person anyway. He delighted to see things historic being put to use.'

As for Lord Gort, 'He enjoyed the idea of banquets,' said Tom Sheedy. 'He enjoyed going down to the gallery overlooking the hall and watching the people enjoying themselves; and he would go down to the basement at the coffee stage and mingle with them. He was always thrilled when somebody might identify him.' On 29 March 1963 'Mercator' wrote in *The Irish Times* that 'Lord Gort, who began the whole thing by buying Bunratty some years ago... was at last week's rehearsal with Lady Gort and seemed to enjoy it thoroughly. I am told that he eats, drinks and sleeps Bunratty.'

On 14 February 1963 Jack White produced a television discussion on RTE devoted to the subject of Irish monuments. The participants were Lord Killanin, journalist, future chairman of the International Olympics Commission and then a member of the National Heritage Advisory Council, Percy Le Clerc and the writer Frank O'Connor. In his column in the Dublin *Sunday Independent* three days later, O'Connor wrote: 'In my lifetime one famous Irish building – and only one – has been restored:

Bunratty Castle. At once the horrible commercial vulgarisation of "mediaeval dinners" has begun [and] turned a great Irish castle into a Tourist Fun Fair, "A Mick at the Court of King Arthur" as I described it in a television programme some nights ago. At the risk of being called "old fashioned" and "a crank" I should say that the proposed destruction of Fitzwilliam Place[1] and the Paddy and the Pig dinners at Bunratty are, as we say in Cork, "lick alike". Our money restored Bunratty Castle and we are entitled to ask that the use made of it will "add dignity to Ireland", in Lady Gregory's famous phrase.'

O'Connor's outburst provoked a reply on 3 March from Charles O'Malley of Limerick. 'I can assure Mr O'Connor,' he protested, 'that the dinners are not vulgar. I do know that for me and about eighty others who were present when the Limerick Branch of the Wine and Food Society attended such a dinner, the occasion put flesh on the bones of history in a convincing manner... . These occasions are not misusing a building expensively restored and furnished; rather are they helping to carry out the whole purpose behind the project of making the many of our age familiar with the lives of the few of past times.'

O'Connor was given the right of reply in the same issue of the paper: 'The point is that something like twenty thousand pounds of the taxpayers' money has been spent to restore Bunratty Castle as a national monument. In some extraordinary way it has been turned into a roadhouse.' He then put a series of rhetorical questions to Charles O'Malley regarding its suitability as a restaurant, interference with a national monument through the construction of kitchens and lavatories and by whose authority such work was undertaken. He continued: 'I appeal to the other Mr O'Malley, Donough [then, as Parliamentary Secretary to the Minister for Finance, responsible for the Office of Public Works] to put a stop to this nonsense before we are completely disgraced. Need I tell your readers what civilised journalists have already said about it?'

There was more to come. Under the heading 'Mediaeval Banquets and Red Herrings', the *Sunday Independent* of 17 March carried a further response from Charles O'Malley, claiming that a paragraph of his letter had been excised and requesting its restoration, with which request the editor duly complied. 'Frank is a wily old fox who knows the value of denunciation in popular Sunday journalism,' it read. 'We who know Frank need not take his pontification too seriously for we know how frequently his tongue is in his cheek; but I feel that there is a danger that many who read his slanted remarks may be wrongly influenced by them. I have reason to believe that Mr O'Connor has never been present at one of these banquets.' O'Malley then added the further observation that 'Mr Childers, one of our more informed and sophisticated Ministers, was the person who suggested mediaeval banquets and pageants. I do not think he would defer to Mr O'Connor in matters of taste.'

It was, in O'Malley's words, the putting of 'flesh on the bones of history' (and that history confined to 'the lives of the few') that prompted criticism from another quarter. 'In the 1950s we were dealing with a different period and a different outlook,' Marcus Ó hEochaidh said of the restoration. 'Monuments of the seventeenth century were not then protected – they were considered too recent.' They were also considered, by a significant element of public opinion, too alien.

'Anything after the twelfth century wasn't Irish', said Percy Le Clerc; and the recreation at Bunratty of the world of the anglophilic Great Earl served to confirm this conviction. On 19 July 1963, the second reading of the SFADCo Ltd (Amendment) Bill was introduced in the Dáil by the Minister for Transport and Power, Erskine Childers. Since the Shannon company was directly involved in the management and promotion of Bunratty, the debate provided the opportunity for those who questioned the ethos of the whole undertaking to put their views on public record.

'To suggest that anything around Bunratty is typical of Ireland is sheer nonsense,' said the opposition deputy John McQuillan, National Progressive Democrats. 'Deputies may get up and criticise me about this but is it typical even in the very description "in silent Bunratty" – or even the description of the girls who work in it and who are described as hostesses? In any other place, they would be described as waitresses, but here the snobbery has to come in. It would make you sick to think of all the humbug that goes on...' A more focused criticism came from Seán Ó Ceallaigh, representing County Clare in the Fianna Fáil interest – the party then in power. He chose on this occasion to speak in Irish, in the certainty that the minister (in common with some others present) would have difficulty in following his argument.

'*Dhein an tAire tagairt do Chaisleán Bhun Ráithe agus na dinéir mheán aoise a bhíonn are siúl ann,' a dúirt sé. 'Ní dóigh liom go bhfuil ceangal ar bith idir na rudaí a bhíonn ar siúl i mBun Ráithe agus stair an Chláir. Na daoine a lonnaigh san áras sin trá, naimhde do chine Gael a bhfurmór.... . Ag caint air na cuairteoirí meán aoiseacha, tagaid go dtí Aerphort na Sionnaine; sáightear isteach i mbus iad agus tiomáintear iad go dtí Mainistir Choinche. Tugtar blodh staire dhóibh ansin. Ar aghaid leo go hInis annsan agus thar n-ais go Bun Ráithe chun an dinnéar mean aoise bréagach do chaitheamh. Ní bheadh aon locht agam ar an rud seo go léir dá n-abródh an tAire gur "gimmick" a bhí ann chun airgead na n-amadán do thógáil agus déarfinn go mbainfeadh na h-amadáin an taitneamh céanna as. Ba chóir, dar liomsa, moladh do na daoine sin cuart ar Baile Uí Bheachain, Corca Rua go léir, siar go Coill Caoi agus Ceann Léime agus soir go Coill Dá Lua. Do chífís ansan radharcanna áiline a sháródh go mór an méid a chíonn siad ar an dturas a leagtar amach dóibh.'*

In translation: 'The Minister made reference to Bunratty castle and the mediaeval dinners that are being held there. In my opinion there is no connection between what is going on in Bunratty and the history of Clare. The people who were settled in that house then, the majority of them were hostile to the Irish people.... . As regards the mediaeval visitors, they arrive at Shannon Airport, they're stuck in a bus and driven to Quin Abbey. There they are given a bit of history. Back with them to Ennis then and to Bunratty again to eat their phony mediaeval dinner. I would not find any fault at all in it if the Minister were to say that it was a "gimmick" to take the money from the fools and I'd say that the fools would get the same pleasure from it. In my opinion it would be right to advise those people to pay a visit to Ballyvaughan, the whole of Corcomroe, west to Kilkee and Loop

Head and east to Killaloe. There they would see beautiful sights that would greatly surpass those that they see on the trip they are allowed to take.'

These, as it happened, were the only dissident voices raised in the course of the debate; and they were criticising what had by then become a sucessful commercial – and professional – operation. The decisive step had been taken with the appointment, in March 1963, of ten hostesses selected out of 640 applicants. 'They will meet the passengers arriving and conduct them on the tour through Co Clare,' the *Limerick Chronicle* reported, somewhat inaccurately, 'ending with the mediaeval banquet at Bunratty Castle. Here, the girls will be expected to join in helping to create the 15th century atmosphere, and for that reason consideration was given to girls with ability to sing or provide entertainment.' 'The couriers were a different group of girls,' said Cora Ryan, who became one the castle entertainers in the summer of 1963. 'They just sat at the banquet with the people they'd have on the bus during the day. I think their job was tougher than ours.'

The task of filling Brendan O'Regan's prescription that 'They would be really fine specimens of Irish womanhood and they would be still able to carry on both the entertainment and the serving,' was entrusted to a selection board made up of Jack Ryan, O'Regan's right-hand man in Sales and Catering, Ray Joyce and Maeve Fitzgibbon, the press officer, 'because', said Joyce, 'we felt we had to have some female protection. We interviewed a series of very lovely young ladies, well-educated, most of them talented... . The quality in those days was terrific because job opportunities weren't great.' 'Brendan had advised me,' said Peadar Lamb, who also had a say in the selection, 'that it was more important to have a person who is a good mixer and a person who indeed might have a good family background.' He was, he concluded, not wanting to be snobbish, but was concerned 'to give the whole thing a high profile. They were very good mixers and they made the guests feel particularly at home... . All the people there worked extremely well together: there was a great team spirit about it.'

'All the girls selected are members of prominent families,' the *Limerick Chronicle* assured its readers: 'Two are well-known harpists who will lend authentic colour to the castle. They are Finola [*sic*] O'Sullivan... and Miss Elizabeth ('Bobbie') O'Brien.' It then listed, with background details, the names of the others: Una Kelly, Maura Roche, Ann Harbourne, Judith Mahony, Joy de Burgh O'Brien, Lelia Maguire, Jacqueline Doyle, and Mary McElligott, 'the only Shannon girl selected'. They were to be instructed in make-up and deportment by Madam J. Chineling of Paris, in elocution by Peadar Lamb, and in local history by Eric Moroney NT, Sixmilebridge.

'There was a Fionnuala O'Sullivan who played the harp extremely well, Peadar Lamb remembered. 'There was Joy de Burgh O'Brien who sang well and did recitations and there was a girl called Mary McElligot from Limerick who performed well there too... . And there was a local man who used to take the guests round on a tour of the Upper Hall and the Americans used to find his accent very fascinating because it had the gutteral 'r' – the French 'r' – in it... . This man Packie who used to take them round, sure they used to find him fascinating when he'd talk about "the tapestries are mostly late fourteenth and early fifteenth century and inside here in the kitchen you see a clock which has no minute hand because in those days only the hours mattered."' Packie the guttural Frenchman was better known as Pa Crowe.

'You greeted the guests when they arrived and just chatted while they had a welcoming drink,' said Cora Ryan, 'and then they were brought down to the banquet, were seated, and you served them. And you entertained them during the meal. I was a singer.' If not one of the very first intake of hostesses, she followed hard on their heels. The first fully public banquet took place on 1 June 1963, the month she was sitting her Leaving Certificate at Coláiste Mhuire in Ennis, and she 'started directly after that and just stayed on'. She had had no formal singing training – 'I sang in the choir at home' – but the ubiquitous Brendan O'Regan had heard her and she was invited for an interview in the Shannon Shamrock with Vincent Dowling of the

*Elizabeth (Bobbie) O'Brien marries at Bunratty in 1968, attended by the Castle wolfhound. In the background, the as yet unreconstructed 'Dirty Nellie's'.*

Below left: *Joy de Burgh O'Brien, of the first group of Castle Entertainers*
Below right: *Fionnuala O'Sullivan, also among the first group*

Theatre and then at Shannon with Jack Ryan. 'When I joined,' she recalled, 'the programme was set and I just moved into it. You picked your own solos and as long as they fitted in with the period and that, then that was fine.'

Cora Ryan's day began at four in the afternoon. After the banquet she would get a lift home with the photographer who took pictures of the guests ('if you wouldn't have a boyfriend collecting you!') or go into Shannon with the other girls on the special bus and get the ordinary bus home to Ennis, arriving at about one in the morning. As a local girl she did not avail of the free accommodation and subsistence provided for the other hostesses in the new flats on Drumgeely Hill, the nucleus of what was to grow into Shannon Town. Between banquets – the venture proved such a success that a second at six o'clock was soon introduced – the girls could eat at the Shannon Shamrock Hotel and use the pool. The food for the castle came from the airport kitchens: 'soup and then the capon and the syllabub. You literally just put big bowls on the head of the tables and they helped themselves.'

The girls' costumes, basically Elizabethan, had been in the experimental period largely a matter of trial and error; but when the banquet became fully professional they were largely modelled on designs in *Costume Cavalcade*, a Danish publication, and executed by Kotchie Bourke, a member of the well-known Dublin family which also supplied, in Jack Bourke, a mayor of Limerick. 'Our measurements were taken and they came back. We had several different types,' said Cora Ryan, 'and we had special costumes for touring. We wore heavy velvet in the castle or heavy brocade and we'd a lighter material for travelling – paler colours.' 'The Ladies of the Castle must in practice combine the qualities of ladies and servants,' Frank McNally wrote in *The Irish Times* on 10 November 1993, 'and their dress is therefore another compromise – elegant enough to be lady-like and light enough for what is a very hard night's work.'

The scene had been set – a scenario created which was to endure, in spite of several half-hearted attempts to tinker with the successful formula. In his novel *In Guilt and in Glory*, published in 1979, David Hanly, who worked with Bord Fáilte before becoming a successful broadcaster and whose book is in many ways a somewhat loaded indictment of the tourist industry, sets a scene in 'Cranmore Castle', highly evocative of Bunratty: 'The great hall was crowded, and the late arrivals got a muzzy image of hundreds of silver-haired men and blue-haired women. Here, in this ancient castle of the O'Briens, the sounds were from Boston and Philadelphia and Chicago and New York, alien vowels echoing from the untouched stone walls which had for hundreds of years thrown back the raucous vulgarities, the poems and brazen songs of feudal lords and minions.'

A decade later Ann Morrow, in *Picnic in a Foreign Land* (1989), somewhat more astringently reiterated the theme: 'This evening a bewildered American, James Minto, a mechanical designer from California, is being made honorary Earl. "I am just regular folks", he says, staring myopically through pebble glasses as a crown is pushed down on his thinning hair. A candlelit banquet, "heavy mead", an evening of "Irish culture, music, history and folklore", a quick look at the Brussels tapestry and everyone is sent home with moist eyes after an emotional chorus of "Danny Boy".... . The banquet, indifferent soup and chicken, is presented for "My Lord's approval". A red-haired violinist with a vulnerable face, wearing pink and purple, joins Lady Deirdre to play a haunting O'Carolan concerto. The noble Earl is blowing his nose, he has never had snuff before.'

'But this is supposed to be authentic,' says a character in David Hanly's novel. 'You call this a mediaeval banquet. The real Irish never had anything like this.' The reply, from the entrepreneur Austin Buggy (who bears, it might be said, only a professional resemblance to Brendan O'Regan) both acknowledges the reservations of critics such as Seán Ó Ceallaigh and encapsulates the concept that lay behind the reinvention of Bunratty: 'Mr Dineen,' said Buggy, 'in the heyday of this castle the people you insist on calling the real Irish lived in wattle huts, wore goatskin knickers, and passed their days hunting and eating gruel. We could have built a few wattle huts and dressed people up in goatskin knickers and hoped that the tourists would flock to them and enjoy the smelly discomforts. But tourists, particularly from your country, while they love to think of themselves as going native, actually like to go native with central heating, air conditioning and showers. Very difficult in wattle huts. So we renovated the castle. The people who owned and inhabited this place from its earliest days were just as Irish as the real Irish you are so anxious about.'

Faithful commemoration or 'commercial vulgarisation'? Drama or deception? 'A curious sense of reality' or...? *'Le panache, le sens de l'humeur et le prodigieux don théâtral des Irlandais,'* concluded *Paris Match* on 23 July 1966, *'font chaque soir de cette réconstitution, qui ailleurs aurait pu tourner à la mascarade, une piece de théâtre un peu irréelle.*[2]

## Notes

[1] In spite of vociferous protests from many quarters extending over several years, a row of Dublin Georgian houses, an integral part of a unique 18th century streetscape, was destroyed by the owners, the State-owned Electricity Supply Board, in May 1965.

[2] 'Every evening the panache, the sense of humour and the great theatrical gift of the Irish make of this reconstruction, which might otherwise have tended towards a masquerade, a somewhat unreal drama.'

# Jousting in the Canaries

T
HE REALLY FINE specimens of Irish womanhood settled quickly into their role, and almost as quickly stepped beyond it. 'Brigid Fitzgerald – she was one of the first girls,' Cora Ryan recalled, 'and she married an American in the first year whom she met at the banquet. Bobby O'Brien married an Australian sheep farmer. You got an awful lot of mothers proposing on behalf of their sons back home: "You'd be so right for my boy". Several times I had that situation.' But Cora Ryan married the manager of the Old Ground Hotel, Ennis, where she was rehearsing in the Leamaneh Hall for her part in the entertainment planned for Dun Guaire Castle, the first clone of Bunratty.

Even before reconstruction there was finished, O'Regan had been seeking new mediaeval worlds to conquer. 'We went out to Knappogue and like this place originally it was that high in dung,' Peter Donnelly remembered. 'We used to take packed lunches and go out to these places and sit down and eat them and look around and try to visualise what might happen and how it could be done.' Both Knappogue and Dun Guaire were acquired and revitalised on the Bunratty model. Dun Guaire opened in 1966 with a literary script by the writer and broadcaster and co-founder of the Dublin Pike Theatre, Carolyn Swift.

At a meeting at Shannon airport on 9 January 1962, Lord and Lady Gort had agreed to a proposal for the combined operation of Bunratty and the planned Folk Park and for the apportioning to Lord Gort of an area of ground to be acquired by SFADCo.

Albert McCarthy, the builder of the Shannon Shamrock, who owned the land, had agreed to sell, but by February of the following year had become impatient with the lack of progress and threatened to withdraw the offer: 'During the last year the Company was permitted freely to use the [Shannon] cottage in connection with the one-day tour,' Peter Donnelly informed the Secretary of the Department of Transport and Power, 'but this year obstacles are being put in the way.' He requested the department's permission to purchase the land for £3,350 approximately. On 13 March 1963 an advisory committee was set up comprising Brendan O'Regan; Andrew Devane, whom he had appointed architect of the Folk Park; John Hunt; Kevin Danaher of the Folklore Commission, who was to have a major input into the new venture; Sean Merry, Clare County Engineer; and Christy Lynch, then manager of Bunratty. The support of Bord Fáilte was successfully canvassed.

Such theme parks have since become commonplace and the target of critics who stigmatise them as tourist kitsch and the Disneyfication of history; but, as with Bunratty itself, the Folk Park was in 1963 close to being a pioneering venture – certainly in the Irish context. 'We realised that we had to keep expanding things,' said O'Regan, 'that one castle alone with the mediaeval thing wasn't going to bring people down out of the skies, and I sent Joe McElgunn and Andy Devane to see St Fagan's [the Welsh Folk Museum] and they came back and made a report on that and Andy did an outline sketch for the Folk Park.'

Seven exhibits were originally planned and, as with the castle, firm parameters of authenticity were to be established. Concern for the integrity of Bunratty's surroundings, as distinct from the building itself, had already been expressed. On 9 July 1962 Cian O'Carroll of Shannon Development had written to the brewers Walter Smithwick objecting to the sighting of a sign reading 'Have a good TIME in Limerick' (TIME was the short-lived brand name of a beer) on the left side of the castle. 'It does clash somewhat with the scene,' he suggested. No reply was recorded. But from the inception of the Folk Park 'certain principles were adopted and rigidly adhered to throughout', wrote Christy Lynch in 1967.[1] 'In the first place it was decided that the exhibits should be replicas of houses in the Shannon region; secondly, they should be entirely authentic in representing Irish country life in or about the first decade of the present century; and thirdly, the presentation should be warm and alive, avoiding as far as possible the static presentation popularly associated with a museum.' The planners were fortunate, wrote Lynch, in obtaining the services of a builder, Thomas O'Halloran, 'who was not only an expert in his trade but also familiar with traditional building methods, and to his knowledge and skill the authentic accuracy of detail is largely due'.

Two methods of breathing warmth and life into the concept were adopted. The first involved the staffing of the forge with a working blacksmith and the dwelling houses with a *bean a' tí*, who baked bread on the open hearth, performed other housewifely duties and chatted to visitors. 'A thatched house is not complete without a woman and a good fire,' as Pa Crowe put it. The second stratagem was the institution of evening entertainments in one of the cottages in the form of a '*Céilí Night*'.

The Ladies of the Castle, as they came to be called, worked for the first two years only in the summer season. 'They were given leave of absence in the winter with half pay,' said Ray Joyce. 'it was a very attractive deal.' In the course of these first two winters Cora Ryan was invited by Vincent Dowling to appear in the traditional Abbey Theatre Christmas pantomime: Peadar Lamb, she recalled, was prince to her princess. In the third winter she stayed on in Bunratty and performed in the Folk Park in a programme that involved her in both singing and Irish dancing, supported by Joan O'Reilly – who was to be her bridesmaid – on the fiddle and Peadar Ó Lochlainn on the uileann pipes. This, again, was an innovation that was to prove its worth.

By the winter of 1966 the entertainers had already gained a reputation further beyond the castle walls. An appearance on an early 'Late Late Show', participation in an Irish Night in the Albert Hall, London, and the first of the overseas tours which were to prove both a promotional and an artistic success had brought them to the attention of a wider audience. The first tour, to the ASTA (American Society of Travel Agents) convention in Miami, took place in the autumn of 1964. 'We had a week in Miami which was absolute bliss,' said Cora Ryan, 'because all we had was about a half-hour show per night and we had all day free – we never got it as easy again.' 'It was the talk of the convention and we couldn't fit the people in,' Ray Joyce, who accompanied them, remembered. Future trips took the girls (the Entertainers for these purposes were all female) all over the United States, performing for Mayor Daly of Chicago, for Cardinal Cushing, and having their photograph taken with President Lyndon Johnson round the desk in the Oval Office. Back in Ireland, they were invited to the American Embassy in Dublin in June 1963 to perform for the visiting President J. F. Kennedy.

In 1966 the Castle Entertainers made a record of some of the most popular items from their repertoire. On the album sleeve photograph, reproducing the banquet setting, are to be seen Fionnuala O'Sullivan, Joy de Burgh O'Brien, Una Kelly, Mary McEvoy, Mary McElligot amongst those of the early intake. Cora Ryan, though not in the picture, features on two solo tracks. Of the many who followed in the pioneering footsteps of that first group, a not inconsiderable number were to go on to success in similar or related fields in the wider world. Bunratty had created an opening for young professional actors and musicians, said Ray Joyce, 'and the experience has stood to many of them. It's a difficult professional job because there are no footlights between you and the audience.' Thirty years on, Cora Ryan looked back on the experience from the performer's point of view: 'It was a lovely, easy, innocent, pleasant evening. It was fun.'

The success of the banquets prompted the managing company, SFADCo, to plan for the provision of a visitor reception centre and new entrance building to the west of the castle. At SFADCo's request, wrote Marcus Ó hEochaidh, 'the National Monuments Branch, OPW, undertook an examination of the archaeological interest of the area west of the castle which was followed by an archaeological investigation on behalf of the company'. Work began, under his direction, on 19 March 1964. Large deposits of soil, clay and gravel which overlay the filled-in castle moat and the newly discovered mediaeval gardens were removed and used to provide a new area of amenity ground and to safeguard the newly laid out courtyard of the castle from possible flooding. On 23 May Percy Le Clerc wrote to the SFADCo secretary, Peter Donnelly, that 'the discovery of the moat and entrance causeway during the digging of the foundations [for the new building] is of particular interest'. It was agreed that construction work should be suspended and that Ó hEochaidh should spend a further two weeks on the site.

The discoveries led, in fact, to a continuous programme of archaeological work which was to continue under his supervision until 1967. 'We had a big team,' he said. 'We had approximately ten students at a time and about twenty-odd workmen; and large areas of the moat had to be excavated and examined.' The OPW were, however, about to embark upon work at Ballintubber Abbey, County Mayo, and Ó hEochaidh found that he had to divide his time between the two sites. 'Childers was down to open the bridge [1964] and said "I welcome the National Monuments Branch of the OPW – all two of them!" That didn't go down too well with the Commissioners... . Le Clerc continued on then with the landscaping of the Folk Park on the basis of my excavation.' In the course of this a second and earlier bawn wall was discovered. 'This led to a certain amount of confusion which still exists,' said Ó hEochaidh, 'because the reconstruction was done piecemeal while the excavation was in progress; and during lulls in the excavation the maintenance team would start conserving what was found and sometimes the interpretation varied, as one would imagine.' Marcus Ó hEochaidh and Percy Le Clerc resigned from the Office of Public Works, within a week of each other, in 1970, and the reports of their investigations remained unpublished.

In July 1963, with the restoration of Bunratty completed and the mediaeval banquets an assured success, the parliamentary secretary to Erskine Childers, Minister for Transport and Power, wrote to Shannon Development, the responsible semi-state body: 'It has been represented to the Minister that yachts approaching the Castle from the Shannon via Bunratty Creek would be considerably facilitated if a mooring quay with steps down from the water were provided downstream of the [new] bridge. At present it appears that yachts can tie up at the old turf quay at high water but that at low water they have to moor in the centre of the stream and that it is somewhat difficult to board a dinghy in order to reach a yacht from the shore.' Sadly, the minister's suggestion was not acted upon, and with the 1992 realignment Bunratty's historic maritime dimension was finally nullified. The view from the battlements is in this respect a poignant one, the great castle lying beached behind its three stone and concrete barriers – one of which is now virtually redundant – its river accessible only to rowing boats, a concrete slipway scarcely comprehending the memory of bustling quays, of the comings and goings of Norman and Irish, Gael and Gall, through turbulent centuries.

Imitations of Bunratty were not long in appearing. Brendan O'Regan recalled one in the Canary Islands 'where there's a pageant, very brilliant horse-riding, and there's battles and joust-

*Excavation of the moat. The figure conveys an idea*
*of the scale of the work.*

ing and so on and the meal is being held at the same time.' In 1979, on the back cover of *The Irish Contribution to Australia*, the proceedings of a seminar published by the Office of the Commissioner for Community Relations, Brendan Locke and Bob Wignall advertised Bunratty Castles in Sydney, Melbourne and Canberra: 'Those of our NOBLE LORDS AND LADIES who have visited Ireland in the last decade will instantly know that we have fashioned the Banquet at BUNRATTY CASTLE THEATRE RESTAURANT on that which takes place nightly in the Fifteenth Century BUNRATTY CASTLE situated in the serene county of Clare.' A decade earlier, in March 1968, Loren W. McCannon and William F. Farrell, of the Long Beach Public Transportation Co, Long Beach, California, had proposed to build a facsimile of Bunratty and suggested that they would like to make some arrangement 'with the Irish Tourist Bureau [*sic*] and the original castle management for promotion that would be mutually advantageous'. The proposition came to the attention of the Minister for Transport and Power, Erskine Childers, whose secretary

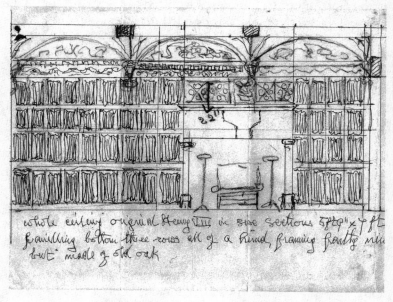

*Lord Gort's sketch for the furnishing of the South Solar*

tartly informed Peter Donnelly that 'The Minister is not disposed to regard the proposal favourably. He is concerned that the creation abroad of replicas of Bunratty Castle which would be linked with your Company's tour and banquet would tend to create a bogus atmosphere around the whole Bunratty project.'

Lord Gort, said J. C. Lynch, was always afraid of too much commercialisation. 'It's really a kind of live museum and he wanted it kept that way,' Peter Donnelly explained, 'not just an investment for making money.' There was 'the danger that after we had all gone other people would start having banquets at all hours of the day and night, selling geegaws etc. So I wrote a memo to the Board recommending that the ownership should be put into another trust separate from SFADCo, which would have some authority over what could be done.'

It sounded simple, but the due legal process was to extend over a long number of years. One of the difficulties, said Donnelly, lay in the fact that Lord Gort, who was childless, feared that the castle would fall into the hands of the trustees of all the Gort interests. Bunratty was vested in Lady Gort, but, said Christy Lynch, 'she eventually decided that she wanted the castle and the collection left to Ireland. But in doing that the legal people on the Gort side felt that there might be difficulties with the heirs afterwards... so what they decided to do was that the building should be sold for a nominal sum to Shannon Development, who would be the custodians, if you like.' The sum involved was £10,000 and the indenture was signed, sealed and delivered on 17 October 1969 by the Right Honourable Bessie, Viscountess Gort, and by Brendan O'Regan representing SFADCo; other signatories were John Hunt, the solicitor John Gillman and Lord Gort. It was not, however, until 3 June 1987 that an indenture was made establishing a trust under the terms of which, as stated, 'The trustees shall hold Bunratty Castle upon trust for the State... to the intent that Bunratty Castle will be preserved in the public interest and made available to the public as a contemporary National Monument. Bunratty Castle may be used as a tourist amenity and as an entertainment centre provided such use is subsidiary to the object aforesaid and provided all profits (if any) therefrom are applied exclusively in the furtherance of the said object.'

One trustee each was to be nominated by SFADCo, Bord Fáilte, the Trustees for the time being of the Furniture Trust and Aer Rianta, the State airports authority. In the matter of management, the Trustees agreed to 'enter into a lease with the Company [Shannon Development] whereby Bunratty Castle will be leased back to the Company' Under the terms of the agreement regulations regarding times and prices of admission were to continue to be made by the Commissioners of Public Works, subject to the approval of SFADCo and the trustees of the Furniture Trust. This latter, created by a deed dated 12 June 1959, had been altered and added to by a further deed dated 3 October 1967 made between the Commissioners of Charitable Donations and Bequests for Ireland – 'the ultimate owners', according to Peter Donnelly – and the trustees; the former body was now empowered to 'make any alteration to or variation of or addition to these presents' by the Building Trust.

Lord Gort had, in a somewhat bizarre ceremony, immediately handed back Shannon Development's £10,000 cheque representing the purchase price of the castle to be applied to the Furniture Trust; and, said Christy Lynch, 'I would look for permission from the trustees and buy bits and pieces.' The South Solar had by now been vacated by the Hunts and he was anxious to help Lord Gort in realising his plans for it. Gort, he said, 'was always saying that it should become an Elizabethan room and he was forever sketching what the room would look like on paper. He had bought linenfold panelling from some early building and that was all stored at Bunratty. He had a ceiling for the room, an Elizabethan ceiling, and unfortunately the ceiling arrived at Bunratty and was stored over a long weekend in one of the outsheds of the Golden Vale cottage and the building went on fire... And I was really very depressed over the whole thing and he was down in the dumps as well because it was a very good one. But, strange enough, there was one panel of the ceiling that remained in England – there was work to be done on it – and he was able, over a number of years, to have the ceiling copied from this one panel. And really I could never tell the difference afterwards. Lord Gort died before we ever started work on the South Solar, but I collected all his little sketches that would be done on paper, leaves of books – he'd leave them thrown around – and from what he had left I was able to restore the room as I thought it should be done... . I was sad he was never able to see it. But I always got the feeling that he was around and his spirit was hovering around the place; because he loved it very much.'

Lord Gort, known to his intimates as Kerry, died in 1976, and with him the direct family interest in Bunratty. His wife Bessie had predeceased him in 1972. After her death, her portrait, by the society painter Philip de Laszlo, was collected from Hamsterley Hall by Christy Lynch and hung in the South Solar apartments they both loved so much. With some difficulty and a certain amount of persuasion in the matter of acquiring a respectable suit for the occasion, Gort himself was induced to sit for its companion, painted in a harmonising style by James Le Jeune and hung next to that of his wife. The South Solar rooms have been preserved as they appeared during the time the Gorts occupied them in the 1950s, a small tribute to their memory and to the magnitude of what they accomplished.

Those who attended the celebrations, on 5 November 1993, to commemorate the thirtieth anniversary of the banquets, found that little had changed. The guests were still served four more or less mediaeval Removes: Smoked Samon [*sic*], Spynoch and Orange in Broth, Allowes in Hony and Gyngere Sauce, Rost Beef and Buttered Wortes; only the Fifth Remove, Carolan's Irish Cream Mousse, betrayed any serious compromise with authenticity. Similarly with the entertainment which the Ladies of Castle offered: if the concept of traditional music had been extended to encompass contemporaries such as Sharon Shannon, there was still no place for 'When Irish Eyes are Smiling'. On several occasions over the intervening years suggestions had been made for radical change, always to be countered by the argument that the formula worked, as its many imitators have amply demonstrated

– and that in any case the show rarely plays to the same audience twice. The banquet is, in many ways, a concept frozen in time, and as such largely immune from the peremptory urgencies of fashion.

Structurally, too, Bunratty itself has largely stood still. The establishment of the Furniture Trust ensures that items will continue to be added as the occasion offers, both to increase the scope of the collection and to replace those few artefacts that are stolen. In this context iron bars have appeared railing off access to some areas, but otherwise the interior is very much, both in style and spirit, as the Gorts and Hunt (who died in 1976) left it, the timelessness in this case echoing, if with a much greater resonance, the now ritualistic routine of the nightly entertainment. Though conceived by Brendan O'Regan on the basis of their acceptability to an Irish audience, the banquets remain still very much the preserve of the foreign tourist. If Americans continue to provide most of the occupants of the Earl's chair and the dungeon, there is evidence that visitors from mainland Europe are attending in greater numbers. The Irish, for their part, would still seem to regard it, from a distance, as something of an evening in inverted commas; though many of those who come to scoff remain to praise.

For all Gort's disinterested mediaevalism and Hunt's practical scholarship, after the opening Bunratty became inevitably, a focus for tourist development. This did not necessarily argue, however, a cynical pandering to the perceived expectations of the market. John Hunt's replica of an ancient *crannóg* at Craggaunowen, near Quin, County Clare, commenced in 1973, was considered of sufficient archaeological integrity to merit an article five years later in the *North Munster Antiquarian Journal*; the acquisition and development of Knappogue, Dún Guaire and Limerick castles was inspired by the same respect for the historical context as was exhibited in the case of Bunratty; the Folk Park continued to grow in conformity with the original principles of regional fidelity; and the appointment as chief executive of Bunratty Heritage and Banquets of Cian O'Carroll, with a scholarly commitment to heritage and folklore, clearly demonstrated continuity of purpose and that criteria other than the purely commercial were being applied.

In all of these developments the Shannon Development company was substantially involved in the context of its responsibilities for tourism in the mid-west, or Shannon region, and in accord with the pragmatic social idealism of Brendan O'Regan. Knappogue and Dún Guaire trod hard on the heels of Bunratty: the restoration of King John's castle in Limerick had been advocated by SFADCo in 1966 in the wake of their success, and the fact that its realisation had to await the passage of a quarter of a century could not be laid at the company's door. Limerick, however, was a case apart: Knappogue and Dún Guaire were viewed very much as counterparts, or extensions, of the Bunratty concept. If the entertainments were to differ in programe detail and were to experience a greater degree of modification over the years, the groundwork was the same, and both were to prove virtually as durable in appeal as their progenitor.

The Folk Park, from its origins as a virtual addendum to the attractions of the castle, has in some respect eclipsed them, as evidenced by its steady physical growth and its incorporation of Bunratty House, the former Studdert and Russell residence, as the only 'real' building in the complex. Some of its success is undoubtedly due to the universal popularity of this type of theme park: easy on the eye, equally easy on the intellect, with a catch-all commercial element and within an apprehensible time-frame. Skilfully managed, the Folk Park has grown big and self-contained enough to be judged on its own terms, so that it is not even necessary to try to relate to its overshadowing castle in terms of replicating the village that for centuries, in one form or another, lay under its walls. In any case the time is out of joint: by the 19th century, the chosen context of the Folk Park, Bunratty had degenerated into the dead heart of a community which no longer owed it any meaningful allegiance.

At the end of it all the one sure thing that can be said of the rebirth of Bunratty is that things will never happen quite in this way again. Sometime during the course of the restoration the archaeologist Ruairi de Valera said to Percy Le Clerc, 'It looks to me as if in the future we'll have no archaeology but a lot of Bunrattys.' He was wrong. Bunratty happened because of an unlikely collocation of aptitudes and interests in a climate which permitted the realisation of highly individualistic aims. Since then the whole scene has changed: politically correct archaeology would prescribe conservation – of all the material from all periods; the obfuscations of the planning process would militate against the individual initiative; and – perhaps crucially – the contemporary cost of the enterprise would place it beyond the reach of all but the most affluent Lord Gorts of this world. Their modern equivalent, the ubiquitous European Union officials, would be unlikely to be caught with smuggled artefacts under their ganseys.

This, it must be said, is not necessarily a cause for lamentation: *autres temps, autre moeurs* – or, in Flann O'Brien/Brian O'Nolan/Myles na gCopaleen's version, other Toms, other Moores. Bunratty, after all, gains much from its discernible uniqueness. In terms of marrying an imaginative entertainment to an heroically restored and refurnished castle it occupies a position, both nationally and internationally, from which – as long as its management retains the integrity insisted on by its restorers – it is unlikely to be dislodged. *Si monumentum requiris...*

---

[1] 'The Bunratty Folk Park' in *North Munster Studies*. This collection of essays was published in commemoration of Monsignor Michael Moloney, who had been actively involved in support for the Bunratty project.

# Bunratty Castle Section Drawing

1. The Great Hall. The original banquet hall and audience chamber of the Earls of Thomond.
2. The Main Guard. The main living room of the common soldiers and the Earl's retainers, it is now used for banquets.
3. Public (Lower) Chapel.
4. South Solar. The guest apartments.
5. North (or Great) Solar. The private apartment of the Earl and his family.
6. Private Chapel.
7. Earl's Bedroom.
8. Earl's Kitchen.
9. Captain's Quarters. Named for the Captain of the Guard.
10. Basement. Used as a store room or stables.

# Further Reading

*The background literature relating to such an extended period as represented by the successive castles at Bunratty is obviously vast, and the following offers no more than a number of starting points from which those interested in delving more deeply may direct their reading.*

Andress, K. R., N. P. Canny and P. E. H. Hair (eds), *The Western Enterprise*, Liverpool 1978.

Cosgrove, Art, *Late Mediaeval Ireland, 1370-1541*, Dublin 1981.

Craig, Maurice, *The Architecture of Ireland*, London and Dublin 1982.

Danaher, Kevin, *Irish Country People*, Cork 1966.

Fitzgerald, Brian, *The Geraldines*, London 1951.

Fitzgerald, P., *The History of the County and City of Limerick*, Dublin and Limerick 1826.

Fitzpatrick, Brendan, *Seventeenth Century Ireland: The War of Religions*, Dublin 1988.

Frame, Robin, *Colonial Ireland, 1169-1369*, Dublin 1981.

Frost, James, *The History and Topography of the County of Clare*, Dublin 1895.

Gilbert, J. T. (ed), *The History of the Irish Confederation and the War In Ireland (1641-9)*, Dublin 1882-91.

Healy, Elizabeth, *Bunratty Castle & Folk Park*, Bunratty 1991.

Le Clerc, Percy, *The Restoration of Bunratty Castle*, Rome, 1979.

Ludlow, Edmund, *Memoirs of Edmund Ludlow Esq.*, Vevey 1698.

Lydon, J. F., *The Lordship of Ireland in the Middle Ages*, Dublin 1972.

Lynch, Christopher, *Bunratty Castle*, Dublin 1984.

McLysaght, Edward, *Irish Life in the Seventeenth Century*, 3rd ed, Shannon 1969.

*North Munster Antiquarian Journal*, Vol. XX, 1978: Studia in memoriam John Hunt.

O'Brien, D., *History of the O'Briens from Brian Boroimhe AD 1000 to 1945*, London 1949.

Otway-Ruthven, A. J., *A History of Mediaeval Ireland*, London and New York 1968.

Penn, Granville, *Memorials of Sir William Penn*, London 1833.

Rynne, Etienne (ed), *North Munster Studies: Essays in Commemoration of Monsignor Michael Moloney*, Limerick 1967.

Share, Bernard, *Shannon Departures*, Dublin 1992.

*The Other Clare*, Vol. 1, Shannon 1977–.

Watt, J. A., J. B. Morrall & F. X. Martin (eds), *Mediaeval Studies presented to Aubrey Gwynn SJ*, Dublin 1961.

Weir, Hugh, W. L., O'Brien, *People and Places*, Whitegate 1983.